KT-104-035

A strategy of change

With its accessible new approach to the key problems of modern strategic management, *A Strategy of Change* is an essential resource for today's MBA student and practising manager who require more than 'instant fix' recipes to deal with the complex problems of strategic change.

The book provides a critical appraisal of current ideas about 'organizational culture', 'total quality management', 'flexibility' and 'excellence', drawing upon case material from a wide range of different organizational settings. This practical, issue-centered approach contrasts with the functionally oriented way in which management is often taught in the classroom and reflects instead the real needs of managers who have to work and communicate on a cross-functional basis.

Dealing in an integrated way with the full spectrum of strategic change issues, this book provides an important tool for all those concerned with organizational survival in the changing environment of the 1990s.

David Wilson is Senior Lecturer in Organizational Behaviour at the University of Warwick and Director of the Warwick distance learning MBA programme. He has published and researched widely in the fields of Organization Theory and Organizational Change. His previous publications include: *Top Decisions* (1987), *Managing Voluntary and Non-Profit Organizations* (1989), and *Managing Organizations: Text Readings and Cases* (1990).

The Routledge series in analytical management
Series editor: David C. Wilson
University of Warwick

This series is a welcome new resource for advanced undergraduate and post-experience students of management who have lost patience with 'off the shelf' recipes for the complex problems of strategic change. Individual series titles cross-reference with each other in a thoroughly integrated approach to the key ideas and debates in modern management. The series will be essential reading for all those involved with studying and managing the individual, corporate and strategic problems of management change.

A strategy of change

Concepts and controversies in the management of change

David C. Wilson

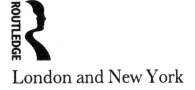

London and New York

First published 1992
by Routledge
11 New Fetter Lane, London EC4P 4EE

Simultaneously published in the USA and Canada
by Routledge
29 West 35th Street, New York, NY 10001

Reprinted 1993, 1995
Reprinted by International Thomson Business Press 1996

© David C. Wilson 1992

Typeset in 10/12pt Baskerville
by Solidus (Bristol) Ltd
Printed and bound in Great Britain by
Mackays of Chatham PLC, Chatham, Kent

British Library Cataloguing in Publication Data
A catalogue record for this book is available from the British Library.

Library of Congress Cataloguing in Publication Data
A catalogue record for this book has been requested.

ISBN 0–415–05326–9 (hbk)
ISBN 0–415–05327–7 (pbk)

Contents

Figures

Tables

General introduction

This book, and the series of which it is part, emerged from a number of diverse sources. Primarily the intention was to write a series of books which would help those interested in organizations at the advanced undergraduate, postgraduate and post-experience levels to view the field critically and holistically rather than from a strictly functional perspective. Like many books, this one originated from a sense of dissatisfaction and from an ambition to create something relatively new in the field of studies in organization. Dissatisfaction sprang first from the predominantly functionally oriented way in which management was taught in the classroom, which contrasted with the way in which those who taught (and who were managers) at this level talked to one another on very much a cross-functional basis. Second, the nature of studying organizations had begun to focus on project work, which required analysis at the interdisciplinary level rather than from a single subject perspective.

Yet the teaching of subjects remained largely functionally based. This was especially true of MBA syllabuses, which, having introduced the 'core' functional subjects, spent the greater part of the year in options which took each core subject to deeper and more specialized levels. Most courses, however, were completed by way of a project which demanded a rather different perspective. Many projects demanded that managerial and organizational problems be examined in a relatively holistic way, necessitating the blending of previously disparate subjects. For example, marketing problems had to be set alongside those of production, and it seemed that organizational structure and culture somehow always had to be considered alongside the financial and accounting issues.

Such simultaneity demands that the examination of organizational issues is both integrative and analytical. Yet it seemed that there was also a pattern. Broad themes emerged – competitiveness, strategic change, internationalization, the nature of technologies, to give some key examples. It was also striking how few texts approached the subject from these perspectives, preferring to keep within the bounds of specialisms. In one of my own 'specialist' areas, for example, the literature on organizational change seemed often characterized by its insularity. Only readers with a background in psychology could appreciate the finer details of organizational development, whilst other change management texts were often academically barren, offering the advice of apparent best practice to eager readers. There are exceptions, of course, but these studies were few and usually pursued in depth only by especially dedicated students. Most MBA students never encountered the critical complexities of organizational change in the texts they read, although they certainly appreciated the debates and the dilemmas when they came to produce project work in the area. Many of the good projects were attempts at synthesizing disparate functional approaches and contradictory theoretical arguments. Whilst the quality of these attempts varied, they were virtually all superior in analytical quality and depth to many of the source texts specializing in the subject. Conversations with many colleagues confirmed that this was the case in a number of subject areas, and the seeds of the present series were sown.

The aim of the volumes in it is to be analytical, critical and thematic. They are designed to help students view organizational issues from an integrative and critical perspective. They are intended for the top-flight MBAs, advanced undergraduates of Business Studies, and practising managers who are not content to remain within the bounds of uncritical and often recipe-bound thinking. It is assumed that readers will have a thorough knowledge of the basic 'disciplines' taught in most business schools and departments of management in universities and polytechnics. The themes chosen are those of internationalization, change and technology, and an attempt is made to link them together under the broad rubric of organizational strategy. These are the first set of themes, and they reflect current concerns which have emerged during the authors' teaching of management in various universities. It is intended that further themes will be added to the series as teaching programmes and the series progress.

Although the style of each volume will inevitably differ between authors, each tries to achieve a set of common goals which should characterize the series overall. First the reader is introduced to a description of the key debates and critical issues in the broad terrain; second, authors take a critical look at current work in the field; third, authors have been asked to assemble the arguments very much from their own perspective so that they follow a particular line of enquiry or reasoning throughout. The intention is to allow readers to follow the debates to help or inform their own perspective. The volumes are not, therefore, teaching texts in the traditional sense, although they should be a useful source of reference for the key debates in various areas. Taken together, they present a wide picture of organizational issues which should, hopefully, inform, stimulate and develop thinking in the broad field of management studies and education.

Chapter 1

A strategy of change: outlining the terrain

Early in my career I was employed by a relatively small organization which specialized in shipping freight, imported and exported from overseas. For those with long enough memories, this was just one year before the introduction of containerized transport (which is now a familiar sight on road and rail heading to and from various ports). Before containers, most freight was crated or boxed, often in a large number of separate items. Containers allowed the bulk carrying of goods which could roll off the lorry and roll straight on to the ship. Ro-Ro technology, as it became known, had distinct advantages in reducing handling costs, securing economies of scale, and making the jobs of driving, delivering and security much easier.

The firm invested heavily in container technology and the business began to grow. There was only one major problem. Whilst it was possible to reorganize the shipping organization internally to cope with the new tasks and responsibilities demanded by using containers, coping with HM Customs and Excise proved a difficult task. Internally, within the firm, everyone was familiar with broader nature of the business. It was also a small enough organization to allow flexibility in jobs during the change to containerized technology. Everyone mucked in together. Customs and Excise, however, still demanded a detailed and itemized list of the contents of containers bound overseas. They had always required this information, and with smaller crates and packaging it was a bureaucratic chore but one which was not difficult to do or to check should queries arise. Customs and Excise provided a huge manual which listed all types of goods, each coded with an individual number. For each type of goods a code number had first to be found, then recorded (in multiple copies) prior to departure for its ultimate destination. With the use of containers the task became increasingly difficult. The loads were greater in volume, more complex and often contained new materials not always to be found in the manual. Loads were delayed whilst recording was completed. Often arguments over the precise nature of the load would arise. How was a particular newly developed chemical powder to be classified? Precisely what was the intended use of the timber? How were particular pre-formed fabrications to be recorded? Were they completed goods or not? Each item had its own separate code. No load could leave without being coded.

The characteristics of this situation can be found replicated in virtually all organizations, from the smallest charity to the largest multinational business. Technology (in this case) had been the engine of change. Parts of the shipping and transport sectors had welcomed the new technology and embraced it as a way of increasing business and profit. Other parts of the business sector had not changed at all, still requiring the new technology to subscribe to the old control mechanisms designed to administrate yesterday's business. Each could produce very plausible reasons either to change or to retain the *status quo*. It took a long time for this business sector and its constituent organizations to reorientate and to rethink around the change. In frustration, many able individuals left the shipping organization, which still had to employ a clerk to record the old Customs and Excise code numbers whilst queues of container trucks built up. Competitor organizations entered the business and any first-mover advantage gained by my firm in the early days was substantially lost. Eventually all organizations in the sector 'caught up' with the change, and containerized transport is now efficient and taken for granted (like so many new technologies).

This story is merely one instance of the 'resistance to change' so forcibly spelled out in textbooks of organization theory and behaviour. In this case, however, resistance came not so much from individuals in a single organization as from one organization which was part of a business sector. In order to describe the resistance to change, it is necessary to shift the level of analysis away from individual employees and individual firms and to focus upon inter-organizational relationships. This multi-level analysis of change processes is neglected in much literature on organizational theory, which seems to prefer, for the most part, to focus on rather individualistic, psychological explanations of resistance to change.

Furthermore, strategies of organizational change have recently become a byword for maintaining success and creating competitive performance in complex organizations, irrespective or whether they provide products or services, or of whether they are privately or publicly owned. The topic of change has also become imbued with a substantial overlay of normativism. Organizational success has become directly attributable to its ability to handle and sustain strategic change. This is a pity, since such recipe-book thinking detracts from the complexity and necessary analytical sophistication for characterizing change. It also overlooks a great deal of empirical and theoretical work which is central to the understanding of organizational change. This book examines current thinking critically and looks again at some of the perhaps forgotten and overlooked aspects of the topic which permeate a number of theoretical perspectives. These perspectives include disciplines ranging from the interpersonal skills of individuals to the strategic management and economic performance of organizations and business sectors.

Currently the topic of change seems ubiquitous. The title of the book, therefore, may seem at first uncontentious. It would seem reasonable that, given the self-evident context of change, most individuals responsible for the strategic direction of their organization would have a 'strategy of change'. Managers should become (if they are not already) 'masters of change' (Thorne 1991). Indeed, much of the current vogue in management theory is for delineating the steps through which successful change can occur, ultimately seeking to generalize from the particular. Instances of a handful of 'successful' processes are proposed as generalizable templates for models of change (Plant 1987; Kotter *et al.* 1986; Peters and Waterman 1982; Kanter 1983; Thorne 1991).

The vocabulary of change management appears to have reached something approaching standardization across much management theory and practice. Developing the 'flexible firm', decentralization, creating 'lean' management structures, the explicit articulation of 'mission statements', 'empowerment' and the development of individual 'competences' to manage these organizations are part of the common parlance of theorists and practitioners. At first sight the consistency of this vocabulary looks encouraging, not least since it appears that academics and practitioners are, for once, speaking the same language. It could also be taken to signify consistency within debates on organizational change. The same words and terminology appear to have the same meaning to all who deal with them. If this were so, then the whole area of scientific enquiry would have taken a substantial step forward.

Yet there is a puzzle which would seem to deny that such progress has been achieved. The puzzle is that the close interest shown by academics and practitioners alike in organizational change has produced an apparent homogeneity of both theoretical vocabulary and applied approaches. Deeper analysis of the evidence which informs such thinking, however, would induce an opposite opinion. All is not homogeneous in the camp of change. Indeed, there are intense debates between virtually all who lay claim to being analysts of change, to the extent that many theories and much empirical evidence appear mutually exclusive. This conflict provided the stimulus for writing this book, so as to explore the conflicting viewpoints emanating from various schools of thought.

The strength of apparent agreement on organizational change should not, however, be dismissed lightly. It has fundamental implications both for academic research and for economic-political relations between business schools, government and the business community. It could be said that there has arisen a whole 'business' of organizational change itself. There are a number of areas in which this consistency may be seen:

1   The increasingly close links between business schools and industry mainly focused upon management training. Training for change has become one of the key elements of training, encouraged by government, with a focus on fostering entrepreneurship, leadership and teamwork skills.

2   The emergence of Human Resource Management (HRM) as a specialism in its own right (and as distinct from Personnel Management) has been recognized both within business schools and in a wide range of business organizations in all economic sectors. In particular, the increasing part played by HRM specialists at the level of the board in many companies is indicative of corporate commitment to change through people.

3   The increasing attention paid to developing individual managers in structured training frameworks aimed at securing a set of predetermined competences deemed to be necessary in creating and managing the new flexible firm and in sustaining the capacity for change.

4   The apparent re-emergence of certainty, and the process of management as a science, reminiscent of Taylor's (1911) 'one best way' of organizing. Today this certainty has arisen in a different guise from the original studies of scientific manage-

ment. In place of Taylor's various efficiency-based routines, the 'one best way' now proposed lies along more structural and cultural lines. The favoured model propounded by many business schools and practised in many large companies is that of the decentralized structure coupled with a task or project-based culture. This requires managers to work increasingly in multi-disciplinary teams; to become generalists as well as functional specialists; and to develop a specific set of competences and skills.

The language used to describe this state of apparent harmony is striking in its unreflexive nature. There is an almost total absence of any sort of critique in much of the literature. All seem agreed on the one best way to organize. Yet how can we be so certain? The relative paucity of empirical evidence available to us (especially that which examines the in-depth processes of strategic change) does not warrant such uniformity, nor the striking levels of normativism which have emerged over the last decade or so. We might do well to remember that Taylorism was an equally potent management recipe, embraced by passionate devotees, but was ultimately to prove troublesome to organizations, which experienced increasingly, severe labour problems, and to Taylor himself, who was asked before Congress to account for the demise of American productivity despite most large organizations having embraced his version of scientific management.

Each of these points will be explored in this book. They form its general thematic approach and guide its logic. Of necessity, in a book this size, there will be a process of selectivity at play determining which themes and which topics are to be covered. This is not, therefore a 'reader' in change management. Nevertheless, the issues outlined above allow the exploration of a wide range of literature which has borrowed and adapted theoretical and empirical approaches from a variety of disciplines. The crucial issue is to confront the terrain which lies along a continuum marked by two extreme perspectives on strategic change. On the one hand are management 'recipes' which provide outright normative maxims for managing change in complex organizations. On the other, there are the more analytical and theoretical approaches aimed at understanding the complex processes of change as an end in itself.

THE ORGANIZATION OF THE BOOK

The aim of the book is to provide the reader with a guide through the variety of analytical perspectives on the understanding of organizational change. To achieve this, multiple perspectives on organizational change are examined, together with the range of metaphors they use to describe the change process. This introduction attempts to illustrate the range of simplicity and complexity, relativism, normativism and voluntarism or determinism to be found in the extensive literature on the subject. The aim is to be as comprehensive as possible in the coverage of change theories, but at the same time the pursuit of a particular set of themes will inevitably colour the 'pure' description of many approaches. The book, then, can be viewed on at least two levels: first, it should provide a useful summary of key approaches to date; second, it develops a specific line of analytical thought which should allow the reader to reflect upon his or her own perspectives on organizational change.

First, we examine the difficulties of approaching the subject of change, given that its very nature is often transient, intangible and, above all, appears to be processual. Change occurs over time. It cannot occur independently of any form of temporal measurement. The degree, nature and extent of temporal measurement are, however, an issue of some debate. Some authors (for example, Pettigrew 1985, 1990a) argue that organizational change can be understood only in the context of large blocks of historical time. Others (for example, Wilk 1990) argue that change is largely non-processual and cannot, therefore, be charted through various phases of historical time. From this perspective, change appears relatively instantaneous (although it does seem to have a historical set of precursive events). As Wilk says:

> Change is not a process, nor is it ever a task, operation, performance or activity ... the mythical view of change as taking time to occur can give us part of the traditional picture in which change, however revolutionary and even dizzyingly swift, is seen as actually happening gradually, step by logical step, rather than occurring by means of an all-or-none leap.
>
> (Wilk 1990: 15)

We shall return to this debate later in the book. For the moment it is sufficient to note the intense level of disagreement between those who argue that change is a drawn-out process and those who deny it. It is also worth noting at this stage that the conception of time used by many authors is not always the same. This is explored in chapter 2.

Second, the book outlines the range of approaches which have been developed by theorists and practitioners for understanding and explaining organizational change. These include *behavioural* approaches, largely derived from interpersonal and social psychology; *structural* approaches to change, which include concern with organizational design and with organizational–environmental linkages and functioning; and *cultural* approaches to change, which regard organizational climate, ideologies and prevailing beliefs (culture) as pre-eminent. It will be apparent that all aspects of change can be examined from one or more of the behavioural, structural and cultural perspectives.

THE IMPORTANCE OF CHANGE IN ANALYSING ORGANIZATIONS

Organization theory has long recognized the topic of change as an important sub-discipline in its own right. Concepts of and approaches to change permeate virtually every aspect of organizational behaviour and organizational analysis. Organizational behaviour has emphasized the roles of training, interpersonal skills, organizational development, communication and effective groups (to name only a few) in achieving and sustaining organizational change. Organizational analysis has tended to emphasize the key role of processes such as strategic decision-making, the exercise of power and the importance of organizational structures in preventing or achieving change. Organization theory has warned against approaching the question of change as if it were an objective 'fact' of organizational life and has proposed that, like many organizational issues, change is predominantly a perceptual phenomenon, understandable only in terms of individuals' accounts of definitions of the situation. It is with these theoretical debates that we start.

The leitmotiv of modern management theory is that of understanding, creating and coping with change. The essence of the managerial task thus becomes one of establishing some rationality, or some predictability, out of the seeming chaos that characterizes change processes. Practitioners and some management theorists seem almost obsessed with the topic. Far from being a leitmotiv within a wider frame of reference, change has become for some the opus itself. It is characterized as the master key to corporate success and competitive advantage (Peters and Waterman 1982; Peters and Austin 1985; Kanter 1983; Morgan 1989). All organizational 'success' factors are anchored in the concept of change.

For others, the challenge of producing models of change has become a preoccupation. For example, Lewin (1951) produced the *force field* model, in which change is characterized as a state of imbalance between driving forces (pressures for change) and restraining forces (pressures against change). Balancing these forces means that no change can take place, since the forces are in equilibrium. More recently Plant (1987) has proposed the *need, commitment and shared vision* model. This is a more specifically managerially oriented model, aimed at helping individual managers steer their chosen change through the labyrinth of the organization. Many others can be found which are derived from such perspectives. Yet, before we explore the utility of such models, we should pose two questions:

1   Upon what intellectual basis (or bases) are models of change constructed? What are the assumptions and what are the prevailing theories in use? What are the definitions of change that are used? What is the degree of supporting empirical evidence? In short, how do we know what we think we know?
2   Has one set of theories or one particular approach greater empirical support than others? Or are some approaches specific to particular kinds of organization, such as non-profit-making, co-operative, public-sector or manufacturing, for example?

These fundamental questions form the basis of the first part of this book. In order to understand change, it is important to locate it within the wider context of meaning, theory and empirical evidence. It is worth noting at this stage that change is a relative concept. That is, when we talk of organizational change we really mean the degree of change taking place rather than assuming that change is the antithesis of some assumed stability. Every phenomenon is subject to change, however apparently stable its nature. This is true in the physical as well as in the social sciences. For example, temperature varies, moisture evaporates or is soaked up, ageing and entropy take place, metals become fatigued, yet over a few hours of clock time each would appear to be enduring and stable. The same is true of organizations. Many appear to remain unchanged over a number of years, yet they are constantly evolving in time, sometimes by accident, sometimes by design. Physically the organization may look the same. For example, many retail stores such as Woolworth and Marks & Spencer remained virtually unchanged in outward appearance from the 1930s to the early 1960s. It is only relatively recently that their appearance within and outside has changed. Yet to work in Woolworth's in the 1960s was a totally different experience (wages, types of jobs, types of technology, etc.) from working there in the 1930s. Things had changed slowly but surely. Thus the degree of change is an important concept. This is one of the first themes developed in chapter 2.

However, the pursuit of individual themes alone in a book of this sort is likely to lead to a fragmented picture. We would have no way in which to relate separate themes one to another, nor even to suggest possible relationships between them. The primary task of any analysis is to develop some framework in which the various themes can be placed and examined in relation to each other. This analytical framework will also serve as a guide when we come to discuss the various models of change which lie along the continuum outlined above. Such a framework allows comparative analysis. Of course, frameworks themselves are not constant. At best they are guides (rather than axiomatic) and, no doubt, any number of frameworks could substitute for the one used here. However, the analysis described in fig. 1 allows us to allocate various theories and models of change along two broad dimensions, which are themselves derived from fundamentally different philosophical approaches to the sociology of organizations.

The four categories in fig. 1 represent an immense divergence across theoretical, empirical and epistemological issues. As with any four-cell box, we should be careful to guard against assuming that the whole world of organizational change can easily find a home in one of the cells. We should also note that none of the cells is a discrete entity, comprising a finite number of specific theories. Change is far more complex than that. Yet the characterization is a useful guide for organizing thinking about approaches to change and it also forms the broad route map for reading this book.

On the vertical dimension, change can either be *planned* or can *emerge* in organizations. Obviously, those models of change which assume that change can be planned in advance will differ radically from those which assume change emerges as a result of the interplay of multiple variables. On the horizontal dimension, change can also be described primarily as a *process* or primarily as a strategy of *implementation*.

	The process of change	The implementation of change
Planned change	**1** Logical incrementalism and various need, commitment and shared vision models	**2** Reducing resistance to change (e.g. force field analysis)
Emergent change	**3** Characteristics of strategic decisions: political process models	**4** Contextualism: implementation is a function of antecedent factors and processes

Figure 1.1 A characterization of approaches to organizational change

Thus in cell 1 the kinds of approaches we would expect to find would make two assumptions. Change can be planned (by managers) but requires analysing in a processual way (i.e. over time). The planned change could be, for example, a reorganization of an office or a department. In this case it would appear that the desired change can be stated in advance. Subsequently other people perhaps need to be convinced of the utility of the reorganization, and the dominant managerial task becomes that of persuading individuals to accept and support the change (see Plant 1987). Managers can also decide in advance the degree of change they wish to bring about. They may decide to 'play safe' and work towards a set of planned changes in small steps, a process known as logical incrementalism (Quinn 1980).

In cell 2 the assumption is still that changes can be articulated in advance, but the emphasis is now that the primary task of change management is implementation. Lewin's force field is a good example of this, since it requires individuals to specify in advance the desired change as well as to decide which driving or restraining forces can be removed to facilitate its implementation.

Cell 3 contains those approaches which view organizational change as an emergent phenomenon. Change is the result of the interplay of history, economics, politics, business sector characteristics (for example). Whilst individuals can still depict future desired states, to understand fully where the vision comes from and how change eventually happens requires an explicitly processual lens through which to view the action. Examples of such analyses would include the works of those authors who accord primacy to the political interplay of powerful factions in organizations trying to get what they want out of the change (see Hickson *et al.* 1986).

Finally, cell 4 introduces the concept of contextualism. The argument is that whilst organizational power play may sway change one way or the other, what is most important is to see the context in which those powerful interests were built up and now operate. The way in which antecedent factors play a part in shaping the current situation is also the stuff of contextualist approaches (see Pettigrew and Whipp 1991). It should also be evident that there is no firm demarcation line between cells 3 and 4, and the degree to which political models of change deal with the contextual aspects of implementation is really a continuum.

Depending upon which perspective(s) are taken, different issues will surface as important to the understanding and management of strategic change. Each perspective varies not only along the dimensions shown in fig. 1 but also as to which levels of analysis are adopted. By levels of analysis we simply refer to the idea that strategies of change can be applied to individuals, to groups, to organizations, to business sectors and ultimately to whole economies and nation states. For example, a great deal of research has recently been devoted to developing negotiating, interpersonal and management style skills for individual managers. In essence, this research (and consequent management training) is aimed at the individual level of analysis, at increasing managerial skill in handling change. It is also aimed at reducing the probability that other individuals in the organization (who are affected by the proposed change) will resist it. If we were to place this example within the framework of fig. 1 it would appear in cell 2, since it falls predominantly under the banner of the *implementation* of *planned* change. It is also at the individual level of analysis. The direction of change has already been decided. The strategy is to manage or neutralize resistance to its implementation.

The shift from emergent to planned models of change has been sure and steady over the last decade. Managers have been encouraged to adopt an entrepreneurial style in order to realize the planned vision. Recent emphases on the management of human resources (both from business schools and from in-company training) have testified to the importance of the manager being able to convince others that the vision of change is correct. Much 'pop' psychology has been revisited in an attempt to 'teach' the skills of interpersonal fluency, leadership and social graces within the business context.

The problems with this approach to organizational change are many. First, it ignores the political and economic context in which most individuals and organizations operate. The assumption is that managers alone can make the difference between achieving and not achieving change. Second, its logical outcome is to reinforce the subordination of non-managerial staff to the wishes of management – except that in this case the wishes are termed 'visions' of change. The language of planned change has a seductive capacity all its own. Fundamentally, planned change models are steeped in the reinforcement of managerial control. They rely ultimately upon the manager being able to persuade, to insist or to cajole others into accepting (sharing) the managerial goal or vision (Plant 1987). Uncritical acceptance of the manager as both agent and sole determinant of organizational change has arguably been one of the enduring features of the last decade or so. Whatever was wrong – inadequate management training: the alleged imbalance between manufacturing and services; unwillingness to invest in new technology – managers could be taught how to remedy the defects, achieve change and bring about a new state of affairs.

Of course, planned change relies upon a model of organization in which there is uncritical acceptance of the managerial role. This appears to be particularly true of North America and Great Britain. A survey of management education (*Economist*, 2 March 1991) concluded that managers in the USA and UK needed to concentrate on the 'softer' areas of people management in order to achieve organizational change. Deeper investigation reveals this to mean that managers are assumed to have an unquestioned basis of hierarchical power. From this, change can occur if managers learn to lead, motivate, negotiate with and dominate other parts of the organization (subordinates and recalcitrant peers). Furthermore, the locus of change is assumed to emanate solely from the management cadre, and the task of implementing it, equally, to lie solely with managers. There is, perhaps, a certain irony in the tasks of leadership and motivation being deemed 'soft' in this context. Leavitt

(1991: 4) argues that management education aimed at achieving such managerial skills transforms 'well-proportioned young men and women ... into critters with lopsided brains, icy hearts and shrunken souls'. The role of management training is discussed in chapter 6.

The same survey in *The Economist* revealed that nations such as Sweden and Japan have a very different approach to defining appropriate skills for the management of change. In Sweden, for example, the law of co-determination means that the charmed circle of change managers is widened to include workers, supervisors, junior and middle managers. Planned change there requires careful consultation with a wide range of staff and does not assume that the onus of change lies solely with management. Nor does management have an unquestioned power base. In Japan high-flying change managers are not put on the fast track for promotion but have to wait their turn. Equally, ideas for change can emanate from all parts of the company. The emphasis on teamwork and responsible autonomy throughout the organization mean that the links between personal success and managerial success are not so acute in Japan as they are in America and Britain.

The dominant American and British perspectives on planned change make sweeping psychological or managerial assumptions (or both). There is little about the context in which needs, values and beliefs are formed (or manipulated). The emergence of social psychology, especially that genre which deals with achieving success in persuasion and negotiation, has masked the sociological analysis of what is meant by planned change. A more sociological perspective would take subordination, domination and control as its prevailing themes (Salaman 1981). Management seeks to retain its control not only directly through its authority but less directly by defining the context in which changes are conceived, described and evaluated.

Even the so-called 'modern' British and American approaches to achieving change through human resource management strategies can find these criticisms levelled at them. Decentralization, responsible autonomy and team working (often imported from what is considered Japanese best practice) can be seen as fads and fashions at best; at worst they are deliberate attempts to exert and retain managerial hegemony. Barlow (1989) argues that many western human resource management strategies for change are little more than symbolic affairs in which 'dominant power groups ... define reality and manage affairs in their own interests' (p. 499). With regard to training managers to plan and handle change, Barlow argues that its value is limited, because individual career advancement and the tenets of planned change management are in direct conflict. It seems that 'successful types are spotted early on' (p. 505) and that advancement is a very much individually based. 'Flyers are looked at as individuals – not as members of the team which is a very different thing. There are very good team people who are never looked at.' (p. 508).

So much for planning change through teams and project groups. Success in individual managerial careers comes from managing the political system of organization. According to Barlow (1989), success in American and British organizations depends on:

1   Having the ear of senior management.
2   Getting on with your line manager.
3   Being articulate.
4   Moving from job to job very fast (less than eighteen months per task).
5   Appearing successful and effective (no one knows or cares enough to uncover the details of the task). It's all about impression management.

Feldman (1989) reinforces this argument. Planned changes involving the development of decentralized, flexible and innovative firms in the west are largely at the expense of individual workers' autonomy. Workers have to recognize and then fall into line with what is considered legitimate to change by senior management. Tailby and Whitston (1989) draw similar conclusions in their studies of British manufacturing industries and their strategies of change.

SUMMARY

The notion of planned change, on the surface a seemingly rational and eminently appropriate task for managers, is not so unproblematic as it may seem. Care has to be taken to recognize the sociological and psychological assumptions that inform what is planned, by whom and in which ways it is implemented. The example at the beginning of this chapter indicates that perhaps a more contextually specific analysis would be appropriate. Certainly, differences in the analysis of change will be dependent upon a wide range of factors, from differences in business sectors to different nation states.

Yet the notion of planned change should not simply be dismissed on the ground of its apparent academic paucity. It has immense potency drawn from practice. The dominant theory-in-use in British and American organizations is the achievement of planned change through managers trained in specific techniques who can develop special skills to see the change through. This despite a growing weight of empirical evidence which indicates that the analysis of change is best understood in terms of its context and of political processes in organizations (Hickson *et al.*, 1986; Pettigrew and Whipp, 1991). This book explores some of the tensions created by this apparent paradox. First, some of the issues associated with more processual analyses of change are examined in the next chapter.

Chapter 2

Contrasting analytical approaches to organizational change

Before examining the different aspects of change introduced in fig. 1, it is necessary to uncover (albeit briefly) some analytical issues which apply to all considerations of organizational change whether they are concerned with process or implementation, are planned or are emergent. The questions of *time*, *evidence* and *method* underpin virtually all analyses of change. Differentiating between whether change should be analysed processually and understood over tracts of time or as a more structural shift, planned, implemented and readily observable from one state to another, is the tip of this much wider series of debates. One central issue for organizational change concerns the nature of time itself. This leads quite naturally into concerns over method in the study of organizational change. The question of how we are to study change will inevitably depend upon our analytical focus. First, the temporal aspects of change are introduced in brief, leading towards a discussion of evidence and method.

EXAMINING TIME IN THE CHANGE PROCESS

Philosophy, history and sociology are perhaps the three major social science disciplines which have grappled most with the concept of time. These disciplines are also those most relevant to the study of change in present-day organizations, since in-built assumptions about the nature of time and sequence have shaped many theories of organizational change. One debate concerns the 'social construction of time' versus the strict sequential chronology of 'clock' time.

From the perspective of historical analysis, Hallett Carr (1961) argues a strong line against causation. This has relevance both for the understanding of history and for the understanding of change in complex business organizations. In a thorough analysis of historical events ranging from the fall of the Roman Empire to the Russian Revolution he warns against causal determinism, in particular ascribing seemingly unconnected events (i.e. those which do not fit into any seeming pattern of causation or sequence) to chance or accident. As he states:

> we have a real problem on our hands. How can one discover in history a coherent sequence of cause and effect, how can we find any meaning in history, when our sequence is liable to be broken or deflected at any moment by some other and, from our point of view irrelevant, sequence?
>
> Hallett Carr (1961: 130)

One result of an overly deterministic view towards change is the search for 'might-have-beens' – a term used by Hallett Carr to illustrate the processes by which individuals appear to insist upon a causal view of events even in the face of irrefutable and/or ambiguous evidence. Even chance itself becomes a causal factor in the determinist argument. The Greeks, for example, following their defeat by the Romans, consoled themselves with the 'might-have-been' that if Alexander the Great had not died so young he would have overcome the west and Rome would have been subject to Greek rule (cited in Hallett Carr 1961). Here the argument is founded upon a strict interpretation of causality. But for circumstances, the outcome of change and the fortunes of its participants would have been different. There is a linear inevitability central to these arguments shared, incidentally, by a great number of social historians and management theorists (as well as by a number of practising managers).

Whipp (1988) highlights the importance of these debates for understanding change in complex business organizations. Whilst the day-to-day activities within organizations may be seen to occur in line with clock time (hours of work, starting and finishing times, for example) this linearity does not always facilitate the analysis of major change and transformation. Such processes can be understood only within the meanings of a socially constructed frame of reference. This could comprise, for example, the cycle of research, design and development of a new product, such as a car or an aircraft (see Whipp and Clark 1986, for example) or the perceived life cycle of an existing product or product portfolio (Kotler 1988). In both examples, time is a perceived phenomenon, socially constructed by individuals in organizations. Cycles, rhythms and pace within complex organizations are thus socially dependent rather than attributable to particular stages along a linear chronology of time. Therefore the process of strategic change becomes explicable only in terms of the temporal context of the wider social system in which it occurs (Pettigrew 1985 1990a). Chance and ambiguity play their part, of course, but they are not inevitably part of a linear sequence along a carefully regulated temporal path. Chance is not just an unforeseen contingency to be placed in a strict temporal chronology.

The notion of pace (how quickly events seem to occur and move in organizations) is also a key factor, not only in understanding temporal issues, but also in assessing the degree of strategic change taking place. Lowin *et al.* (1971) and Watzke's pioneering work (1971, 1972) distinguishing between 'rural' arenas, where the pace of organizational life is perceived to be regular and relatively slow, and 'urban' arenas, where events are irregular and relatively quick to occur, has direct implications for the study of organizational change. In one sense, this analysis is based firmly upon the notion of market transactions (Williamson 1975). The speed of transactions, measured by clock time, gives an indication of the base level of activities from which change can occur. Change processes are thus anchored to some factor which indicates the pace of transactional activities. The degree of change is derived from the extent to which the existing pace of base-level activities is itself pressured to change. Hawley (1950) and Meier (1962, 1968) refine this overly economic view of pace (through transaction times) into one of socially perceived 'tempo' and 'loci of action'. Their argument is that, whilst it is possible to distinguish between urban and rural arenas, the perception of individuals within each arena of whether tempos of activity feel 'right' is the key to understanding the degree of change occurring within any social context. This concurs with Gerson's view that every setting has its own *a priori* 'temporal order' which is commonly held by participants. The management of change is a 'process of continuing readjustment and negotiation' of this structure of time (1976: 800).

The social construction of time does not simply apply to the level of analysis of the single social system or organization. Business sectors, inter-organizational networks and national societies appear to have their own very different social constructions of time. Anthropologists have long examined the absence of clocks in some remote villages and have noted the different attitudes taken towards 'clock' time among villagers.

Analysts of organizational strategy have also indicated that clusters of organizations within specific business sectors will also display differences in orientation towards time. In some sectors the pace of change as measured by clock time is relatively rapid when compared to other sectors. Yet the perception of the pace of change (i.e. its social construction by participants) may give a different picture (Grinyer and Spender 1979; Grinyer et al. 1987).

In the history of thought itself (how we know anything about change itself) the temporal debate outlined above is central. Foucault's (1973) interpretation of the development of modern thought places both the social construction of time and the analysis of sequence at centre stage. For Foucault the development of modern thought has not been a sequential, linear progress of reason. There has been no successive order of thought and no incremental refinement of ideas through time. Rather, changes have occurred along multiple paths of progress (what Foucault calls 'modes of being') and the essence of change is the process of transformation between such modes, so that one or more forms of knowledge becomes predominant over others.

Such debate raises the funamental question of whether there can be such an identifiable management process as the planned strategy of change. For in accepting the logic of strategic planning (see fig. 1) we are also embracing the notions of temporal linearity and sequence – the cornerstones of planned incrementalism (Quinn 1980). Or is change a rather unplanned process which undeniably occurs but which surfaces in organizations in the same ways as Foucault's modes of being, thus rendering the language used to describe both the process and its assumed causation extremely central, since it is this language which will decide which ontologies and epistemologies surface and take precedence over other forms of explanation and description (Pettigrew 1990b)? The next chapter examines this debate in more detail.

EXAMINING EVIDENCE AND METHOD

The question of evidence comes to the fore once again when we ask the epistemological question: how do we know what we know about change processes? Depending upon the method(s) chosen by researchers, the choice of factors deemed to be important in characterizing the change process differs markedly. First, it is necessary to define the level of change in question. The levels are depicted in table 1. The table 1 identifies the degree of change experienced and separates the degrees into four levels. As the title of this book implies, its primary concern is with levels 3 and 4 (see table 1). These are change processes which are strategic decisions (in contrast to operational decisions) and which require a transformation or shift in the current ways of operating or thinking about the business. This is not to say that the more operational levels of change are unimportant. Doing more of the same, for example, can become a strategic decision beset with problems and discontinuities of its own (Hickson *et al.* 1986). Operational decisions, too, can benefit from analysis of their more strategic counterparts. Consequential and complex strategic change decisions, however, tend to reveal more of the nature of unprogrammed and emergent organizational activities

Table 2.1 Levels of organizational change, classified by degree of change

Degree of change	Operational/ strategic level	Characteristics
Status quo	1 Can be both operational and strategic	No change in current practice
Expanded reproduction	2 Mainly operational	Change involves producing more of the same (goods or services)
Evolutionary transition	3 Mainly strategic	Change occurs within existing parameters of the organization (e.g. change, but retain existing structure, technology, etc.)
Revolutionary transformation	4 Predominantly strategic	Change involves shifting or redefining existing parameters. Structure and technology likely to change, for example

(Pettigrew 1990a) and also afford a firm basis for comparison between the different approaches taken by a wide range of authors on strategic change.

The terrain of strategic change is, however, marked by an immense variety of conceptual approaches, many of which are characterized by their mutual exclusivity. Each approach draws upon its own empirical sources of evidence for support. Broadly, researchers at the strategic level appear to lean towards one of two broad theoretical stances. These can be characterized in many ways, but the brief descriptions below are one way of distinguishing between broad approaches:

1 *The systemic conflict framework.* The organization is viewed as a social system. Because of this, it will be characterized by conflict, politicking and inherent tensions. The tensions can arise between individuals, departments in a single organization or between organizations in larger networks. It is these tensions and contradictions which provide the impetus for change. Energy to support the change process comes from unresolved tensions within the single organizational unit, the ultimate goal being to achieve a new balance between the current set of conflicts.

2 *The strategic choice/entrepreneurial framework.* The organization is still viewed as a social system, but the focus of analysis shifts towards one which embraces the notion of 'strategic choice' (Child 1972). Solutions to perceived problems are assumed to be found outside the organization. The manager's task is to scan the environment and import the most relevant solution. This perspective also views the managerial task as essentially entrepreneurial – the manager as the 'doer', in Peters's (1987) terms.

These two frameworks underpin much of the work on strategic change. Certainly they have guided much current thinking both in management training and in human resource management (see chapter 1). As Armstrong (1989) notes, much of the emphasis in HRM and in management training falls under the rubric of the strategic choice/entrepreneurial framework described above. The role of the HRM and management training is ultimately to produce managers who are more autonomous, more generalist in corporate perspective, more entrepreneurial, managers who view themselves as arbiters of strategic choice (Storey and Sisson 1989; Keep 1989). They are agents of their organization, searching outside its boundaries for solutions and innovations to current problems and practices. In contrast, there appears to have been relative neglect of the systemic conflict framework in which the context, history and antecedents of change are fundamental pieces of the jigsaw of evidence and understanding. Such analyses are both rare in number and inherently more difficult to research, in contrast to studies of managerial entrepreneurialism, management training and strategic choice.

Thus the frame of reference colours the chosen theory (or theories) in use. Below are summarized some of the major organizational theories which fall within either the systemic conflict or the strategic choice frame of reference. The aim is to reveal the extent to which concentration upon one frame of reference will inevitably wholly or partially exclude the consideration of theories-in-use which fall under the other.

Systemic conflict frameworks include the following theories of organization:

1   Contextualism.
2   Population ecology models.
3   Organizational life cycles.
4   General market and business sector approaches.
5   Power in organizations and political models of change.
6   Social action theories (ethnomethodological and dramaturgical – the organization and situation as defined by individuals and the use of metaphor: the organization as theatre, for example).

Strategic choice frameworks include the following theories of organization:

1   Organizational Development.
2   Planned incrementalism.
3   The enterprise culture as normative practice.
4   Entrepreneuralism and intrapreneurialism.
5   Learning from 'best practice' (e.g. Americanization and Japanization).
6   The use of external consultants and change agents.

There are, of course, some theoretical approaches to strategic change which do not fit comfortably in either framework. These include strategic change through mergers, joint ventures and acquisitions (for example, see Harrigan 1985, 1986, 1987) and general contingency theories which deal with organization–environmental interrelationships (see Burns and Stalker 1961; Lawrence and Lorsch 1967).

A primary reason why neither of the above approaches fits neatly under one or other framework is simply that they can be classified as both systemic conflict and strategic choice approaches. For example, an 'organic', flexible and decentralized structure for an organization could be the conscious and proactive choice of individual managers who considered it best practice in rapidly changing and unpredictable markets. It could also be the result of historical antecedents, business context and more reactive managerial decisions towards general changes in the business sector. Equally, a decision to enter into a joint venture could be viewed as both a deliberate decision (strategic choice) and as an emergent process (systemic tension). As Johnson and Scholes (1988) argue, there is nearly always scope for managers to exercise strategic choice, but at the same time there are contextual forces which are determinate and which individual managers cannot change.

This blurring of action/reaction and of evolution/revolution in change processes is important, since it highlights the point that it is not necessarily the theory-in-use alone which reveals it epistemology. It is the use to which the theory is put. For example, contingency theories can provide the basis of a broadly neutral analytical framework (however incomplete or partial) or they can strongly support a set of normative guidelines for organizational change. The distinction between *theory* (which framework is chosen) and *theorizing* (the manner in which the theory is used) allows us to make the difference clear.

The question of evidence, too, will be tied into theoretical perspectives. The level and unit of analysis chosen will vary according to the theoretical approaches adopted. Put simply, if the theory of change demands that evidence is collected about the history of the organization, its socio-economic context and the interplay of organizational power plays over time, then the method chosen for study will inevitably be in-depth and longitudinal. On the other hand, if context is thought to be less important than the attributes of individual managers, the method chosen will focus on key individual managers and their characteristics (such as their personality, leadership qualities, etc.). Between each approach lies a range of methods, each of which gives differential emphases to the roles of contextual or individual factors. The type of evidence generated will also inevitably differ. Cross-sectional studies will reveal far more about the profile of selected variables (e.g. size of organization, management styles, decision styles, personality traits) across a range of organizations. Contextually bound studies will reveal more of the complex interplay of more macro factors over time in one or perhaps a handful of organizations. The relatively quantitative or qualitative approaches to data collection and analysis will also vary accordingly. The main point is to recognize that both theoretical and methodological approaches will not only determine the nature of the evidence revealed but will also influence which factors are selected as important for study in the analysis of strategic change. The remainder of this book attempts to amplify some of these issues and to show how any account of organizational change, or any prescription for change, can best be understood from its theoretical assumptions and beliefs.

SUMMARY

This chapter has outlined some of the underlying assumptions which are inevitably made by those who study and analyse organizational change. Before trying to classify approaches (as in fig. 1, for example) and immediately proceeding to the analysis of change in any organization, it is crucially important to recognize the impact of theoretical and empirical approaches to the topic. Economists, psychologists, organization theorists and sociologists all have their own often contradictory approaches to the same topic. Analysts such as Burrell and Morgan (1979) usefully point out the implicit assumptions made across the social sciences, and one aim of this book is to illustrate how different paradigms of organizational change will inevitably lead towards contradictory conclusions. One important difference is the role of voluntarism or determinism in explaining organizational change. Do we begin to understand change better through the cognitive actions of managers (voluntarism) or through the forces of economics, environment and context (determinism)? The next chapter begins by exploring these contradictions.

Chapter 3

Planned versus emergent change processes

From the previous chapter, it is evident that the extent to which change processes can be viewed as planned or not depends to a large degree upon whether the systemic tension or strategic choice framework is favoured. Of course, these frameworks themselves are derived in part from the much wider debate on voluntarism versus determinism in theories of organization (see, for example, Gouldner 1980; Burrell and Morgan 1979; Reed 1985). Voluntarism (strategic choice framework) emphasizes the role of human agency, whereby 'human decisions can make an important difference ... a voluntarism in which human courage and determination count' (Gouldner 1980: 54). Determinism (systemic tension framework) emphasizes the 'lawful regularities that inhere in things and set limits on human will' (Gouldner 1980: 54).

Determinism includes, for example, the economic structure of societies as one of the prime determinants of organizational processes. This view is expounded in some detail by Burrell and Morgan (1979) in their discussion of 'radical structuralism'. Determinism is also at the heart of many economic theories of the firm, especially those which give primacy to the power of the business cycle over the entrepreneurial manager. This view inevitably brings with it some degree of fatalism. The failure of many entrepreneurs to sustain the changes they have brought about in their organizations has been attributed to wider factors of economic determinism.

A recent example of this surrounds the departure of Sir Ralph Halpern from his position as chief executive and chairman of the Burton Group (he was replaced after resigning by Laurence Cooklin, who became chief executive in November 1990). Halpern had diversified the Burton Group from a predominantly off-the-peg clothing business into travel, transport and property, among other businesses. He was the entrepreneur – the manager with strategic choices at his fingertips. In the short term, diversification brought financial success, but failure in a number of these businesses lead to a substantial drop in group profits. In attributing reasons for the failure market economists were virtually unanimous. Sir Ralph Halpern was overtaken by one of the stark realities of business endeavours, that of the business cycle. The business cycle is created and sustained when separate individuals or organizations make decisions in pursuit of their own interests, without knowledge or consideration of decisions being made at the same time by others. Since the bulk of these decisions use monetary resources, the tendency is for cyclical fluctuations between prosperity and depression for individuals, organizations or business sectors. The entrepreneur falls inevitable prey to the cyclical, deterministic forces of industrial economics.

The power of the economics of the market versus the power of managers to effect change has become one of the key themes of debate in the 1990s. In a special edition of the journal *Academy of Management Review* dedicated to these debates, Bettis and Donaldson (1990) outline the key arguments for an economic theory of organizational determinism or for a more voluntaristic approach in which managerial action is central to the analysis of change. They argue that:

1   Purely economic approaches can explain only some organizational phenomena.
2   This is because economic models of the firm make unwarranted assumptions about individual human behaviour and organizational processes.
3   Management theory on the other hand is too behavioural in its approach, ignoring the 'realities' of the market such as transaction costs and agency theory.
4   Economic views of the firm rely heavily on the concept of material self-interest among actors (firms and individuals). This conflicts irresolvably with behavioural concepts such as the roles of intellect, ethics and aesthetics in explaining strategic change.

The overall finding from these debates is conclusively that economic theory and management theory are unable to transcend their own paradigmatic boundaries. They appear to be mutually exclusive concepts which provide different theoretical frameworks, requiring different analytical techniques, and which are as far apart today as they were over fifty years ago.

The wider sociological debates which fall within the voluntarist–determinist continuum are beyond the scope of this book. However, the central tenets of voluntarism and determinism fundamentally underpin the subject of this chapter. Can managers plan strategically for change? If so, upon what bases do they rest their assumptions and strategic models? Some decisions appear beset by factors which, with hindsight, appear obvious but at the time of decision were apparently not considered. The 1990 Fujitsu–ICL venture seemed set for success yet it has raised questions about the 'nationality' of the new company. Is it British or Japanese? If it is deemed to be Japanese (as is currently the case) then the organization will be automatically excluded from access to the European computer intelligence networks to which ICL previously had unhindered access. (See McKiernan 1992 in this series for a more detailed account of the internationalization implications of change strategy formulation.) In this chapter, the terrain of approaches to change is mapped out broadly under the voluntarist and determinist headings. Subsequent chapters then take a more detailed view of the philosophies of these approaches.

PLANNED STRATEGIC CHANGE: A STRATEGIC VOLUNTARIST CHOICE FOR MANAGERS

In the extreme, planned change strategies would be those processes in which there was a smooth transition from some previously articulated strategic vision towards a future desired state (such as an envisaged portfolio of potentially successful products and services). This extreme and probably unattainable view is, however, the basic principle underlying a considerable amount of change theory and technique, much of which can be found in examples from the North American literature on organization theory and organizational change. (See Kotter *et al.*, 1986, for a collection of such approaches.) The ultimate objective is continuously planned change. The means by which this is to be achieved vary markedly, but include the application of psychological models through organizational development and programmed 'packages' such as Total Quality Management and some management training (see chapter 6).

Planned change through changing the behaviour of individuals

Organizational Development (OD) and Behaviour Modification (BM) represent the two major approaches to implementing organizational change through individuals. Briefly, OD models are founded upon the principle of achieving consensus and participation between individuals in an organization. Change (through organizational growth, for example) is approached in the OD perspective by ensuring that effective participation on the part of individuals leads to consensus among those most affected by the change. The basis of the OD approach is that the attributed cause of difficulties in the change process (i.e. the non-achievement of the desired state) is precluded through poor interpersonal relationships in the organization.

Behaviour Modification is the normative essence of the wider concepts of motivation, reward, learning and organizational culture (which are discussed in more detail later in this book). The change process viewed from the BM perspective is seductively simple. First, managers articulate a vision of which kind of organizational culture they want (based upon available models of culture and upon the assumed strategic consequences of a specific cultural–environmental fit). Second, the process of change is one in which individuals in the organization are persuaded to 'buy in' to the desired culture. This involves modifying the behaviour of many individuals so that they act in line with the demands of the culture (e.g. the expected style of management, behaviour, dress, etc). Third, the technique of BM is put in place to achieve the change process. Based upon Skinnerian psychological theories of learning (Skinner 1961), BM is a systematic approach to reinforce those types of behaviour which are 'appropriate' and to dissuade individuals from adopting behaviour which is deemed to be inconsistent with the achievement of the desired culture. Concepts and models of motivation, learning theories, reinforcement and conditioning are pertinent here, as are issues of management training and development (see Wilson and Rosenfeld 1990). The most obvious difficulty with planned strategies of BM is the extent to which individuals are required to change their behaviour. As Ricardo Giordano (the North American-born chairman of the BOC Group) states with perhaps typical North American brevity and quotability; 'If you're a hands-on guy and someone tells you to take your hands off, you're afraid the car will crash' (*Sunday Times*, 'Business World', 4 November 1990).

Planned strategies of change: improving the analytical ability of individuals

There are a large number of frameworks, recipes and training programmes which are designed primarily to achieve one major goal. That is to help individual managers analyse change, predict the likely consequences and handle resistance and blockages along the way. One such framework, introduced in chapter 1 and familiar to most readers, is the force field analysis of Kurt Lewin (1951). To energize change requires an 'unfreezing' of the *status quo*, the change to be effected, then a 'refreezing' or consolidation of the new state. Lewin argued that organizations exist in a state of equilibrium which is not itself conducive to change. This equilibrium (the *status quo*) is the result of opposing forces which constantly act upon the organization and its individuals. These are forces for change (driving forces) and forces against change (restraining forces). Table 2 shows a typical set of such forces.

Lewin called the process of balancing driving and restraining

Table 3.1 Lewin's equilibrium: driving and restraining forces for organizational change

Driving forces (forces for change)	Restraining forces (forces against change)
New personnel	*From individuals*
Changing markets	Fear of failure
Shorter product life cycles	Loss of status
Changing attitudes towards work	Inertia (habit)
Internationalization	Fear of the unknown
Global markets	Loss of friends
Social transformations	
Increased competition	*From organizations*
New technology	Strength of culture
	Rigidity of structure
	Sunk costs
	Lack of resources
	Contractual agreements
	Strongly held beliefs and recipes for evaluating corporate activities

forces a 'quasi-stationary equilibrium'. A true equilibrium assumes that no change takes place, given a perfect balance between opposing forces. The opposing pressures of driving and restraining forces will combine to produce a quasi-stationary equilibrium – a kind of temporary state of balance.

In order to promote the right conditions for change, individuals have to identify driving and restraining forces. Then there has to be an unfreezing of the quasi-stationary equilibrium. This means creating an imbalance between the driving and restraining forces. Lewin argued that there was an optimal way of achieving this imbalance. First, the restraining forces should be identified and selectively removed. The driving forces would automatically push change forward, since removing the restraining forces would have created an imbalance in the quasi-stationary equilibrium. Ideally, an increase in the number of driving forces or in the potency of the existing ones will achieve a greater degree of change. Refreezing the new situation is the final stage. This sequence is essential, according to Lewin. If extra pressure is put upon driving forces, the result will be an increase in the number or the potency of restraining forces, and the *status quo* will remain.

The force field remains a central feature of many planned change strategies. Although there are many variants, the essence of most models involves training the individual to recognize driving and restraining forces and to take action to manage the balance in the desired direction. For example, Plant's (1987) process of change – collect data, analyse it, create a vision (where you want the change to go), take action and implement change – is largely based on the force field model. A feature of post-Lewin models is that the planned change process becomes increasingly normative. Managers *should* examine what power they have in order to exert influence over the various forces (Plant 1987: 40) or *should* adopt particular inter-personal tactics, depending upon situational contingencies. For example, managers should collaborate with others in situations where feelings and emotions need exploring, or when more inform-ation is needed; they should compete with others when quick decisions need to be made or when others are likely to take advan-tage of non-competitive behaviour (see Thomas 1977: 487, for example). A whole array of appropriate behaviours can be built up once the driving and restraining forces have been assembled within the overall vision.

The seeds were sown for a contingency framework to grow from these models. Dunphy and Stace (1988: 317) argue that planned change can be managed along the lines of identifying key contingencies which gives managers 'a choice of strategies for managing organizational change in different circumstances and for the training of change agents'. The question of management training for organizational change is covered as a separate topic in chapter 6. The Dunphy and Stace framework is shown in fig. 2. The model is heavily based in Lewinism. The addition of an extra variable – whether or not the organization is out of fit with its environment – merely adds to the list of driving and restraining forces. The notion of organizational fit is examined in the next section of this chapter.

On the positive side, the Dunphy and Stace framework does avoid the universality of Organizational Development and

	Simple change (reproduction or expansion of existing state)	Transformational change (changes incurred to existing state)
Collaborate	**1** *Use when:* The organization is in fit but needs fine tuning Time is available Key interest groups favour the proposed change	**2** *Use when:* The organization is out of fit There is little time Key interest groups support radical change
Coerce	**3** *Use when:* The organization is in fit but needs fine tuning Time is available Key interest groups oppose the proposed change	**4** *Use when:* The organization is out of fit There is little time Key interest groups oppose change, but change is central to survival of the organization

Figure 3.1 Change strategies and conditions for their use (adapted from Dunphy and Stace 1988: 331): **1** participative evolution, **2** charismatic transformation, **3** forced evolution, **4** dictatorial transformation

Behaviour Modification approaches. Less positively, it replaces unitary normativism with a fourfold normative choice for managers, giving them the option of adopting incremental, transformational, collaborative or coercive approaches to achieving change. As Dunford (1990: 131) notes, this is merely 'moving from the frying pan into the fire'. Four major criticisms can be levelled at the four-fold model:

1   It is purely normative, with only a little empirical evidence to support the claims for its universality. Dunphy and Stace cite only six examples of organizations in their article. Furthermore, the examples are presented as if chosen to 'fit' the categories already outlined. Thus empirical evidence is not the basis of theorizing but its justification.

2   The model assumes that individual managers will not only have perfect knowledge about different interest groups and their political predispositions in the organization, but will also be able to predict the outcome of actions taken in line with, or against, their defined interests.

3   The concept of organizational 'fit' with the environment is assumed to be unproblematic. Environment is left undefined, and it is assumed that individual managers have the inform- ation to let them see that their organization is out of fit. It also assumes that a congruent fit between the organization and its environment necessarily leads to more effective organizational performance.

4   The model deals primarily with the normative side of imple- menting change and neglects to examine the processes by which the need for change arises and is championed in organizations.

These questions surround not just Dunphy and Stace's frame- work. They permeate a wide range of intellectual tradition. We will explore each question in more detail in this book. First, we examine the concept of organization–environment fit.

Planned strategies of change: the concept of organizational fit

Planned strategies which rely more upon structural and some strategic factors in the organization (and less directly upon individual behaviour) include the process of planned incre- mentalism (Quinn 1980) and the organization–environment 'fit' or 'misfit' approaches. Quinn's planned incrementalism can be viewed as a half-way house between OD approaches and organization–environment 'fit' (Burns and Stalker 1961). Arguing that change can and should be planned in small steps, Quinn proposes a model in which managers gather information from the operating environment of the organization, assimilating it over long periods of time. This information is then disseminated throughout the organization and shared by all individuals, giving the impetus to and the justification for small, constant but evolutionary change. Essentially, a process of democratically agreed, incremental mutual adjustment represents Quinn's orderly, progressive and collaborative view of change.

A further step down the planned, incremental road leads to the relatively well populated domain of the contingency theorists (at least, those contingency theorists who inhabit the terrain of normativism). It seems a little unfair to lay accusations of normativism solely at the well trodden door of Burns and Stalker (1961) or Lawrence and Lorsch (1967). Given the limitations of their respective samples, and the context in which the empirical research was conducted, the links between mechanistic forms of organization and placid, predictable environments and organic organizational forms with turbulent, unpredictable environments seemed plausible and were a good agenda for further research. In neither of the above studies were explicit claims made for the irrefutability of organization–environment congruence. As an ideal type the organic, flexible structure had greater instant normative appeal in North America (following the Lawrence and Lorsch studies) than was the case in Britain (following Burns and Stalker's work). As Lammers (1990: 193) states:

> The main message ... [in North America] has been the propogation of the flexible, organic type of bureaucracy as a way of organizational life beneficial to all stake-holders ... it fits humanitarian values and holds the promise of making people happy and prosperous.

In Britain the logic of economics and systems prevailed to a far greater extent. Understanding the detailed mechanisms of organizational systems became the preferred focus of many organization theorists. In addition, the impact of industrial relations in Britain and the 'negotiated order' perspective they held of the workplace precluded the instant appeal of adopting the decentralized, participative organization as a role model for success (organizational or individual).

At the time of the publication of the Burns and Stalker study (1961) many British firms were experiencing severe reductions in profitability and a loss of competitive advantage both domestically and overseas. Large firms such as ICI and Esso (both with mechanistic structures) sought to negotiate direct with workers rather than change their organizational structure to increase levels of participation. The reasons appear to lie in the nature of the unionized environment facing these and other British firms. The nature of pluralistic trade union–management relations meant that for many managers 'success' could be achieved simply by marginalizing the influence of trade unions over management strategies (see Nichols and Beynon 1977, for example). This was the primary aim of the so-called productivity bargaining agreements. Schemes spawned from these agreements included profit-sharing schemes, job enrichment programmes and joint consultation. However, their spread was sporadic. Many firms, especially in the engineering and manufacturing sectors, retained an almost unchanged profile of management–trade union pluralism. Even the moves towards collective bargaining at the level of the sector (rather than the individual organization) introduced by the Labour government under James Callaghan (1975) proved unsuccessful in achieving integration and consensus within British firms (see Tailby and Whitston 1989 for examples). As late as the mid-1980s ICI was still predominantly a mechanistic organization, with none of the characteristics of decentralization, flexibility and consensus (Pettigrew 1985). In Britain, at least, it seemed as if strategic change through the adoption of organic structures had to be prefaced by attending to the inherent divisions between managers and unions, labour and capital.

More generally, contingency theories of organization–environment congruence are beset by problems of defining what is meant by the term 'organization', but especially what is meant by the concept of the 'environment'. Which factors are included in these terms and which are not? By way of example, Hughes (1985) posits the equally convincing case that the successes enjoyed by Burns and Stalker's Scottish organizations were due as much to the political favour of the government as to the adoption of an 'appropriate' organizational structure. The addition of another political factor into the contingency framework alters the probable impact and causality of variables and certainly questions the immediate nexus drawn between organizational form and success.

Defining the environment poses a key intellectual problem (see Smircich and Stubbart 1985 and Mansfield 1990 for a summary of approaches). Briefly, conceptions of the organizational environment can be summarized as falling into three broad categories. The environment is:

1   An objective 'fact' for individuals, existing external to organizations and readily open to description and definition.
2   A subjective 'fact' for individuals. The environment is viewed as a tangible set of external factors but is dependent in its definition upon the variety of subjective interpretations of individuals. Managers perceive the environment in different ways and they act upon their perceptions, not on any objective 'reality'.
3   Neither objective nor selectively subjective. The environment is 'enacted' (Weick 1979). It acts as an influence upon individuals in organizations but is simultaneously recreated and redefined by them. Thus organizations are influenced by and exert influence over their environment. The notion of a strict demarcation line between the organization and its external environment is no longer taken for granted. Boundaries are permeable and constantly open to definition.

Thus two problems confront planned change at this level of analysis. First, the inherent difficulties with contingency approaches in defining what constitutes the environment or the organization make planned strategic change through these routes a questionable approach (both empirically and theoretically) and consequently perhaps a risky venture. Second, the context in which 'fit' is sought will have an impact. For example, in Britain, factors of industrial relations and the politicization of the workplace cast some doubt over the uniform adoption of fully organic forms of organization either as to be normatively encouraged or as politically viable.

These doubts have done little to dissuade advocates of organization–environment 'fit', however, some thirty years since the publication of Burns and Stalker's original work. Miles and Snow (1984: 10), for example, argue that 'Successful organizations achieve strategic fit with their market environments and support their strategies with appropriately designed structures and management processes. Less successful organizations typically exhibit poor fit externally and/or internally.' The Miles and Snow argument develops, however, to include organizational strategy as the key alignment factor between organizational structure and environmental characteristics. Given a particular portfolio of strategic decisions, organizations are classified as 'defenders', 'prospectors', 'analysers' or 'reactors'. Reactors are the odd ones out. They are organizations with a poorly defined strategy, or which pursue 'inappropriate' strategies for the conditions of the operating environment. Miles and Snow conclude that all strategies apart from the 'reactor' strategy are feasible in a competitive environment, since they are the means by which at least minimal fit is achieved between strategy, structure and environment. Nevertheless, the Miles and Snow strategic analysis is heavily underpinned by the assertion that successful organizations have lean, decentralized and action-oriented structures.

An example contrary to the contingent formulae is the case of Sulzer Brothers, based in Switzerland. Faced with declining profits (66 million francs in 1983 and two further years of losses) the new president of the board, Fritz Fahrini, began to change the organizational structure. For many years the organization had been organic. Decisions were decentralized, managers at all levels were given a great deal of autonomy and decision-making was predominantly by consensus. In less than two years Fahrini began to change towards centralization and bureaucratization. The division of labour, previously blurred and cross-functional, is now very clearly demarcated. Job descriptions and responsibilities were redrawn so as to be much more precise. The ultimate aim is eventually to split the organization into separate product divisions, each run as a separate company bound by common bureaucratic rules. Here the adoption of a mechanistic structure appears to have been successful. Despite poor financial exchange rates, group sales rose 2 per cent in 1987 and group orders increased by 4 per cent in the same year. The first quarter of 1988 saw a 14 per cent increase in orders (Wicks 1988: 6–12).

This seemingly aberrant success might be attributable to the national context (something rarely considered by most proponents of planned change). In Switzerland most managers have a relatively high level of education (particularly in comparison with their UK counterparts). Loans and capital are relatively abundant and cheap. Coupled with an extremely stable political economy, the national context of Switzerland differs markedly from that of Britain and many other European countries. In addition, around 12 of the top 26 Swiss companies are family-owned, so the propensity towards more centralized structures is perhaps not surprising.

Planned change and dominant paradigms

It was proposed in chapter 1 that the field of change strategies had entered a phase of neo-Taylorism. There is 'one best way' of organizing, namely decentralized structures coupled with team-based cultures to foster innovation and entreprenurialism. This view has not occurred by accident. It has emerged through development in organization theory. Dominant paradigms which have emerged during the last decade appear to have fuelled the neo-Taylorist view. Broadly, they include:

1   Learning from and adopting 'best practice', especially that in North America and Japan.
2   The increasing ideological intensity of the 'enterprise culture'.
3   Increased faith in consultants, change agents and gurus of organizational change.

Although it is possible to distinguish analytically between the above areas, they are essentially different facets of the same philosophy of change management. The notion of best practice can emerge only if anchored firmly to a particular culture or school of management theory. In turn, this perspective will define the role of external consultants and will to a great extent determine who is considered an expert or management guru. (Even that terminology indicates specific orientations towards the process and practice of management.) Japanese inventory processing techniques such as just-in-time and Kanban (demand for parts is pulled rather than pushed through the production process, usually controlled by chits or order cards) sit comfortably alongside systems such as Total Quality Management (derived from both Japan and North America) and the tenets of decentralization and 'excellence'.

It is not so much the existence of such techniques and systems that should give rise to caution. It is rather the anti-intellectual context from which they are viewed, which begs questions over the role and efficacy of such management theories in planned organizational change. Such critiques draw heavily on the critical stance taken by Adorno (1973) towards the social construction of 'authentic' knowledge in philosophical thought.

Adorno's point was that all ideologies are essentially the products of social culture. This means that many theories have an assumed authenticity and applicability which is not always justified. His most relevant critique for the purposes of this book is that of German existentialism, where he argues that existentialism was not only a social construction – and therefore also a product of history – but also led to a 'jargon of authenticity' in which meaning and reason were inherently biased, producing a 'mystification of the actual processes of domination' (Adorno 1973: viii). It produced 'an attitude of trustful reliance' (p. 24) in which all philosophies were set within the context of their ideological parameters. Management theory is no exception to the dogma of authenticity.

As an example of what is considered 'good practice' as contextually bound (and therefore open to different interpretations) it is instructive to look at the recent experience in the motor industry of Jaguar and Ford. Prior to the purchase of Jaguar Cars by Ford in the autumn of 1989 (for £1.6 million), Jaguar had been hailed (by academics and practitioners alike) as a model of success for planned cultural change. Of the pre-Ford era Pettigrew *et al.* (1989: 124) said:

> a great deal of the company's performance from 1980 to the present rests on a major shift in the core beliefs and assumptions of the Jaguar management and workforce. The new senior management team from 1980 have not only introduced 500 new engineers, totally recast the existing management, created new purchasing, finance, sales and marketing, and communications departments, and brought out a completely different new saloon model, but they have also given coherence to these differing activities, by creating, or more properly reviving, a common culture . . . the commitment to engineering excellence and quality which had flourished under the Lyons regime . . .

Of the post-Ford purchase era Bill Hayden, the British Ford executive who took over as chairman after Sir John Egan, was quoted as saying; 'apart from some Russian factories, Jaguar's was the worst I have ever seen' (*Economist*, October 1990). Overall, Ford executives felt that Jaguar was inefficient at production. Most other car markers had long ago abandoned the demarcation lines and quota systems which were characteristic of Jaguar, they said. They described as alien such notions as individual responsibility for quality, the use of multi-skilled teams or Japanese-style 'pull'-based inventory processing systems.

The question here is not which account is right or wrong. Rather the point is that the differing accounts of how far down the road of change Jaguar had travelled are a matter of degree and of interpretation. These are coloured in turn by the context in which notions such as 'best practice' are couched. The views of Ford and those of British academics and Sir John Egan clearly do not coincide.

The current context of management gurus, change agents and best practice can be viewed as locked into the central themes of the 'enterprise culture'. Keat and Abercrombie (1990) neatly summarize key aspects of this culture by identifying its central motifs.

Economic characteristics:

1 Continual process of privatization. ·
2 The deregulation of industries (especially financial services).
3 The structural reorganization of publicly funded bodies.
4 A reduction in reliance upon the culture of dependence throughout all organizations and business sectors. This includes reliance on each other as well as upon government agencies for support.

Socio-cultural characteristics:

1 The view of competitive market organization becomes the dominant role model for all others (including public statutory agencies and the voluntary sector).
2 The vocabulary of management theory becomes predominantly that of commercial practice (e.g. 'market niche', 'product differentiation', 'sustainable competitive advantage').
3 A noticeable trend towards the homogenization of organization models. All organizations are normatively encouraged to adopt commercial modes of operation, especially where they are expected to lead directly to increased organizational performance and success.
4 The idea of running even one's own personal life as if it were a business becomes highlighted. Individuals should organize their lives around economic concepts of opportunity cost and operate under norms of overt market competition, for example.

The above is an indicative rather than exhaustive list. Its capacity to set the context in which theories of change are viewed is nevertheless all-embracing. The term 'enterprise culture' describes what many authors have called 'post-Fordism'. Broadly, 'Fordism' (*c.* 1930–70) describes the long period of economic growth associated with this period, with commensurate industrial and economic organization.

Fordism:

1 Organization around the mass production of single products.
2 The economics of mass consumption spur the emergence of large, vertically integrated organizations.
3 The spread of organizations across the country into dispersed, remote site plants or branches.
4 Technologies focused upon single products.
5 Semi-skilled work forces, represented by large general trade unions.
6 Management theories predisposed to scientific management.
7 The need for industrial and economic change, viewed as a natural process of facilitating mass production and consumption.

Post-Fordism:

1 Organization around the production of multiple products aimed at niche markets.
2 Decentralization and the creation of the flexible form become the means to achieve this.
3 Multi-skilled work forces, represented by no-strike agreements or by no unions at all.
4 Organizations concentrated in new industrial sites.
5 Management strategies aimed at achieving the best out of individuals – people are the key organizational resource. Management theories predisposed towards human relations management.
6 The need for change viewed as a natural result of facing up to economic crises and depressions. Planned change emerges as a central managerial task.

Following Jessop *et al.* (1988), the enterprise culture, the era called post-Fordist and the emergence of Thatcherism (1979–90) are seen as closely interrelated. For the theme of this book the label is irrelevant. Of critical importance is the normative influence such a context (whatever its name) has upon the management of change. Firms *should* change towards specialization, subcontracting many areas of production. The move towards this has been termed 'flexible specialization' (see Piore and Sabel 1984). Firms *should* employ multi-skilled full-time workers alongside part-time, contracted and other temporary workers (see Atkinson 1984). Firms *should* adopt decentralized, lean structures and should create organizational cultures which allow individuals to become fanatical adherents of the aims and values of the organization (see Kanter 1989). The management of change thus becomes a managerial prerogative in which the individual manager *should* be multi-skilled, interpersonally expert, psychologically fluent and constantly able to plan for change. The enterprise culture is not simply specific to Britain, but permeates organizational theories in most of the western world.

The origins of these shifts towards defining the manager as a 'change master' (Kanter 1983) have been variously attributed by different authors. Some give primacy to markets and market segments, arguing that increasing instability in product markets leads organizations adopt niche strategies (Piore and Sabel 1984). Others give primacy to technology and its development (see Scarbrough and Corbett 1992 in the present series), arguing that automation, information technology and computer-controlled production have facilitated the emergence of the flexible firm. The result has been a context which supports the belief that planned change is possible; that managers can be trained to manage change; and that a good manager combines entrepreneurial flair, general management skills and a thorough understanding of technology. John Banham, Director General of the CBI, and Hugh Norton, a managing director of BP, have predicted that by the year 2000 one in three British managers will need to be of the above variety (*Observer*, 4 November 1990).

Whether or not we view the above normativism as broadly correct or as 'authentic jargon' depends on the extent to which we support the counter-evidence that change is an emergent rather than a planned process amenable to being directed by managerial technique and action.

EMERGENT STRATEGIC CHANGE PROCESSES: THE WIDER FORCES OF DETERMINISM

The evidence that change processes are largely a function of deterministic forces is broad in both theory and empirical evidence. Yet it is unified by the theme that empowering managers to plan for change ignores the impact of wider and more determinate forces which lie outside the organization and outside the realms of strategic choice for individual managers.

Emergent change processes: open systems and related approaches to organizational change

The Open Systems approach views any one organization as an inter-dependent piece of a much larger whole. Its actions and characteristics are no longer determined just by the aspirations of its managers and founders, but by characteristics of the wider organization–environment linkages. It is the patterning of these linkages and interdependences which enables the deterministic nature of strategic change to be examined (see fig. 3)

It is argued that the Open System perspective allows us to see the following as characteristics (Von Bertalanffy 1956; Emery and Trist 1960a, b):

1 *Equifinality.* Organizations and their managers have a choice over the design of internal organization. There is no one best way of doing things. There are multiple, different ways to achieve the same goal.

2 *Negative entropy.* Entropy is the predisposition of objects to decay and to disintegrate. In an open system this tendency is halted or sometimes reversed (hence the term 'negative entropy'). Organizations import more resources from their environment than they expend in producing outputs. They can 'store' energy in much the same way as some animals survive periods of lean food supply by some form of hoarding.

3 *Steady state.* The balance between inputs, outputs and through-puts is characterized by always being in steady state. This is not a true equilibrium, for the steady state is itself subject to move-ment, but the balance of the exchanges taking place in the system remains steady. There are direct comparisons here with Lewin's force field theory (see table 2).

4 *Cycles and patterns.* Reciprocal and cyclical patterns can be iden-tified. The most obvious is where the revenue from the sale of goods (outputs) is used to purchase further inputs. This would represent a single-loop cycle. More complex cycles can occur where single loops interact, or where tangential factors operate.

In the analysis of strategic change the Open Systems approach allows the variance which occurs within the firm to be explained by factors which lies outside it. It also makes comparative studies of strategic change easier, since all types of organization are argued to operate within an open system.

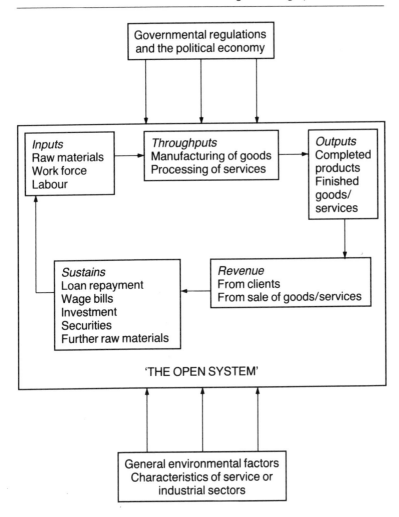

Figure 3.2 The Open Systems perspective: forces for stability and change in the wider context

There are a number of theoretical and empirical studies based in the context of Open Systems which have relevance to emergent and deterministic views of organizational change. Two relevant perspectives are the population ecology and the life cycle analyses.

Population ecology models

The organization is first viewed as one member of a set of similar organizations (the population). Organizational change and ultimate survival are an ecological process in which demands from the environment can result in the demise of 'weaker' organizations and 'select out stronger, more dominant organizational forms' (Bedeian 1987: 9).

> From the population perspective, the distribution of organizational forms at any time is a result of three processes: the creation or birth of new organizations, the disappearance of existing organizations (through death, merger, bankruptcy, or whatever), and the transformation of existing organizations into new forms.
>
> Aldrich (1986: 72)

Strategic change processes are aimed at achieving and sustaining a position within the general population of organizations. Environmental niches and organizational strategies are the key concepts in this process. *Niches* represent the constellation of resources which support or inhibit organizational change. They can be wide or narrow. Niche width is determined by the combination of general resources and factors specific to a particular industrial sector, such as business cycles, product cycles, rates of innovation, union policies, the general economy, government policies and regulations and fiscal trends.

Populations of organizations exist within each type of niche in a way similar to that described by Porter (1980) in his account of 'strategic groups'. These are groups of organizations within one industry or industrial sector which, faced with similar niches, tend to adopt similar change strategies. These patterned strategic change responses have been called 'recipes' by Grinyer and Spender (1979), who noted that organizations which operated in similar business sectors would frequently adopt the same strategies (reorganization, divestment, merger, for example) when faced with pressures for change. Greenwood and Hinings (1988: 294) make the same point when they argue that 'the structural attributes and processes of an organization frequently have a coherence or common orientation, forming an archetype ... giving them an overall "gestalt" or "configuration"'.

Populations of organizations which have a broad environmental niche are those of generalists. They can transform or reproduce themselves with relative ease, since they are argued to have a tolerance of changing conditions and to be able to handle competitors (an argument reminiscent of Burns and Stalker and Lawrence and Lorsch). Specialist organizations are those which have a narrow niche. Such organizations are argued to perform well in environments which are stable or which change slowly and predictably. They have specific resource requirements and usually serve tightly defined markets. They also can build into their structure a great deal of flexibility which also helps in the process of smooth adaptation to changing circumstances so long as change is neither too radical nor unpredictable. (Again, earlier contingency work supports this view.)

In a given population of organizations the pursuit of particular *strategies* by some organizations which differ from sector recipes can temporarily upset the equilibrium of the wider open system. Examples are the more efficient use of the existing resource base, or exploiting and acting upon new information which other organizations in the population have no access. The temporary disequilibrium thus created supports competitive advantage for this organization by facilitating first-mover advantage. This could occur through the entrepreneurial spirit of managers, which is unlikely to be distributed evenly among organizations in the population. The extent to which first-movers retain their competitive advantage is wholly dependent upon how quickly their actions can be copied.

Other sector-based strategies rely upon such aspects as organizational culture and the adoption of new technologies. So long as the mix of structure, processes and people (culture) remains distinctive and inimitable, the organization should enjoy a competitive advantage. In this instance, the strategy of change is thus focused heavily on the management of organizational culture (which is discussed later in this book). Strategies of change through adopting new technologies, or technologies not employed by other organizations in the sector, are very similar to the previous culture example. Where success is associated with the adoption of new technologies, the strategy of change will become technologically driven, characterized by the constant search for and the adoption of new technologies (see Scarbrough and Corbett 1992 in this series).

Organizational life cycles and strategic change

The life cycle perspective gives primacy to the deterministic potency of organizational age and development over time to frame emergent strategies of change. Change is thus a transitional concept, under-standable only in the context of analysing organizations over time. In its most extreme (and normative) form (see Greiner 1972) this perspective argues that organizations adopt evolutionary, incre-mental strategies of change in times of stability (i.e. within distinct periods of organizational history) and revolutionary change strate-gies between different historical periods (e.g. at specific stages in growth or product range and diversification).

The life cycle provides a framework for studying the patterns of birth, transformation and death in organizations (Kimberly and Miles 1980). Each stage provides the context for particular change strategies. Essentially, the life cycle can be viewed as the deter-ministic process of bureaucratization as organizations grow. When formal bureaucratic organization begins to 'fail', the final stage in the life cycle is one of strategic change to break the seemingly inevit-able mould of bureaucracy. A brief, typical life cycle pattern is described below.

1 *The entrepreneurial stage.* In this first (often entrepreneurial) stage, the first task to be achieved is to provide a service or manufac-ture product. Survival is the key strategy. Organizational culture is fashioned by the founders of the organization. It may be a brand-new organization or a new subsidiary or part of an estab-lished, larger organization.

Success brings growth and the need to recruit more staff. Staff need managing, and the question of future organizational strategy becomes more complex. The alternatives are to limit growth and remain small (but risk being unable to sustain competition) or to grow and recruit professional managers.

2 *The collective stage.* The organization begins to take 'shape'. Departments and functions begin to be defined and the division of labour is the dominant theme. The professional managers recruited tend to be strong leaders who share the same vision as the founders. Further growth brings the need for management control and delegation. The organization has begun to establish its position; internal tasks are allocated and who has responsi-bility and autonomy to carry them out become pre-eminent.

3 *The formalization stage.* Systems of communication and control become more formal. There is a need to differentiate between the tasks of top management − to make strategic decisions and to implement policy − and those of lower-level managers, who

are expected to carry out and oversee operational decisions. Bureaucratization occurs as systems of co-ordination and control emerge, including salary structures, reward and incentive schemes, levels in the hierarchy, reporting relationships and formalized areas of discretion and autonomy for lower-level managers. The organization continues to grow, but more slowly. Towards the end of this stage it can become overburdened by the process of bureaucratization and the need for the structure to be 'freed up' becomes pressing.

4   *The elaboration stage.* This is the stage of strategic change. The organization may have reached a plateau in its growth curve and may even show the first stages of decline in performance. Managers used to handling bureaucratic structures and processes usually have to learn new skills to achieve change, such as team work, self-assessment and problem confrontation. This stage may also include the rapid turnover and replacement of senior managers (Greiner 1972).

SUMMARY

This chapter has dealt primarily with the distinction between voluntarism and determinism in strategic change. To a great extent, both these approaches permeate all that is to follow in the book. It is necessary, however, to highlight the extent of conceptual disparity which currently exists between advocates of each, so that what follows can be viewed by the reader in that context. The voluntarist–determinist dimension represents the vertical dimension in fig. 1. The next chapter deals with the horizontal axis, change either as predominantly processual or as a problem of implementation.

Chapter 4

The process and implementation of strategic change

Like all analytical frameworks, the distinction between process and implementation is a necessary simplification in order to clarify some of the apparent paradoxes and alternative assumptions made by theorists and practitioners in the area of strategic change. To understand the *implementation* of change is to place the management (and in the extreme, perhaps, the manipulation) of individuals at centre stage. This means implementing preconceived models of change, all with the aim of achieving a particular set of expected, predetermined and desired outcomes. To understand the *process* of change is to examine critically the context, the antecedents and the movement and history of changes, keeping at the same time an analytical eye on the organization theories-in-use which inform such an analysis. Many authors attempt to span both process and implementation in their work (see Pettigrew 1985, Pettigrew *et al.* 1989, for example). Their argument is broadly that implementation is not solely the logical end point of a process of formulation, but rather the interplay of many iterative and discontinuous factors (including management decision processes, environmental and business sector characteristics, as well as human agency).

It is, nevertheless, the case that empirical data from such contextualist approaches are, as yet, the results of analysing and examining the more processual nature of change and to a lesser extent reflect implementation. This is not surprising, since the examination of context is a huge undertaking which requires a synthesis of understanding of the environment (see the previous chapter), the understanding and characterization of strategic decision-making processes (see Hickson *et al.* 1986) and the characterization of transformation and change in specific organizations. This leaves something of a conceptual gap in which contextualists seek the meaning and characterization of process, whilst those interested in implementation pursue the path of developing 'appropriate' management roles, competences, skills and techniques geared to achieving predetermined objectives. Current work which falls somewhere in between these areas is rare. One exception can be found in Mangham's (1986) metaphor of the management process as a drama, in which managers play out scenes. This 'dramas' illustrate to some extent how roles are contextually derived, yet emphasize that performance (implementation) is the outcome of the learning and the interplay of roles in the current setting. Mintzberg's attention has refocused in the 1990s on a revisitation of the nature of managerial work (Mintzberg 1973), again in an attempt to link current managerial action with past history. At the time of writing, published work is not available. Yet these are fragments in a very large picture. To understand why the implementation–process gap has occurred, it is necessary to consider (albeit briefly) the role of organization theories in explaining strategic change and the limitations they have imposed on the field generally.

THEORIES OF ORGANIZATION: SOME LIMITS ON THEIR ABILITY TO ANALYSE AND EXPLAIN STRATEGIC CHANGE

Whilst the majority of approaches to strategic change find their intellectual roots within the broad church of organization theory, it has not always proved a very fruitful or helpful association. The dominant religion of organization theory (to stretch the metaphor) is that of structural functionalism. The search for general laws of organization in the social sciences corresponding to those of the natural sciences became a preoccupation of organization theorists for around fifty or sixty years. The emergence of criticism within the discipline only began to gather a head of steam some sixty years after the publication of Taylor's *Principles of Scientific Management* in 1911. The orthodoxy of structural functionalism, or the analysis, paralysis and reduction of organizational life to a myriad of variables (Clegg and Dunkerley 1977), has formed the dominant pattern of studies in strategic change. The search for generalized laws of change still pervades the discipline.

Yet other theories of organization offer alternative explanations. The dominant paradigm of structural functionalism led inevitably towards viewing organizations as self-contained entities within which the variables of managerial behaviour could be isolated and identified. Once identified, the variable effects of such varieties of behaviour upon achieving (or failing to achieve) change could be mapped out. The constituent parts of managerial behaviour towards the effective management of change could thus be 'frozen' into a set of recipes, awaiting the microwave oven of application. Thus the implementation of change through the achievement of specified managerial skills (interpersonal, team-building, self-development and management competences, for example) became the inevitable focus of much work in strategic change.

Other theories of organization questioned first the orthodoxy of structural functionalism and, second, whether the management of change could be assembled into a tool-kit of variables. There is insufficient space here to recount the emergence of a critique of organization theory (see Reed 1985 for one such account), but the impact of viewing organizations as political systems, as the mobilization of political and economic biases, as cultural and symbolic institutions, or as systems of social and economic domination, has brought with it different and conflicting views of strategic change. Burrell and Morgan (1979) mapped out the explicit and implicit assumptions of theories-in-use by employing the notion of dominant paradigms. They not only showed the predominance of structural functionalism, but also revealed that some paradigms (largely the interpretive, humanistic approaches) had relatively very little representation in the constituency of organizational research. In a recent analysis of the field, Gioia and Pitre (1990) redraw the Burrell and Morgan four-cell diagram (which allocated each of their four paradigms equal space) in an attempt to show figuratively the predominance of functionalism (fig. 4). Gioia and Pitre go further in their analysis by arguing that the divisions between paradigms are virtually watertight. They do accept that some multi-paradigm approaches can be found, but these run the risk of being in the grey areas between paradigms and thus become neither one thing nor the other; 'paradigmatic synthesis, *per se*, is not possible because of the basic incompatibility of paradigmatic assumptions, vocabularies and goals' (p. 599).

The implications of these arguments for dealing with strategic change are fundamental. Underpinned by a biased, particularistic scientific mode of functionalist logic and analysis, the theory and practice of change have become recipe-driven at best. In the worst case, theories of change rest upon few theoretical foundations, rely as much upon emotional feel as upon rigorous analysis and are

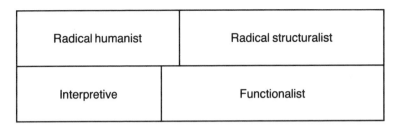

Radical humanist	Radical structuralist
Interpretive	Functionalist

Figure 4.1 The four-cell model of Burrell and Morgan (1979) as redrawn by Gioia and Pitre (1990: 585) to show the dominance of functionalism

characterized by a lack of empirical research. These allegations are also made explicitly in relation to Organizational Development techniques by Strauss (1976), Kahn (1974) and Alderfer (1977).

The emergence of irrationality into organization theory, and with it recognition of the innate impracticability of designing planned change programmes, took place some thirty years ago, when a number of authors pointed out that not only were individuals largely incapable of acting wholly rationally, but also that organizations themselves were institutionally capable of acting irrationally (see Cyert and March 1963; March and Simon 1958). Much irrational behaviour was argued to stem from two sources – uncertainty and political behaviour. These are examined in the next section.

CHANGE, IRRATIONALITY AND ORGANIZATIONAL POLITICS

Mmany of the change models discussed so far are characterized by their relative focus on outcomes and their apparent certainty. For example, the force field model of Lewin (1951), which has informed many subsequent theories, rests upon the certainty that, given an imbalance between restraining and driving forces for change, desired outcomes can be achieved and reconsolidated by rebalancing the forces for and against once the change has occurred. This implies not only rationality on the part of individuals in achieving change, it also necessitates individuals being able to articulate unambiguously a finite list of driving and restraining forces in any particular set of circumstances.

As March and Simon (1958) pointed out, individuals are severely limited in their ability to look beyond a restricted number of possible alternatives, let alone compile a detailed and complete list of driving and restraining forces for change. Lindblom (1959) also demonstrated that individuals tend to seek inspiration from the past in order to guide future action in an attempt to provide some level of certainty. People stick generally to what they know and to use it as a template for future decisions (Braybrooke and Lindblom 1963).

Lindblom's 'incrementalism' represents what he terms a 'real world' description of how organizational transitions are made through the decision-making process. The strategy of change here is one of evaluation, continually building out from the current situation in small steps and by small degrees. Intellectually, incrementalism is justified by the need to match strategic changes to the limited cognitive capacities of individual decision-makers (March and Simon 1958). Pragmatically, it also reduces the scope (and hence the cost) of information collection and computation. Wilson (1980) summarizes the key aspects of incrementalism:

1   Rather than try to survey all alternatives comprehensively, decision-makers concentrate on those policies which differ marginally from existing practice.
2   Only a relatively small number of decision alternatives are considered.
3   For each alternative strategy, only a few possible consequences are evaluated.
4   The decision problem becomes continually redefined. There is no single outcome but rather a series of outcomes which are really numerous means–ends and ends–means adjustments. To rationalize this, individuals often say it makes the problem more manageable.
5   The outcome of incremental change is rarely one correct solution but rather an unending series of attacks on particular problems.
6   The strategy of change is remedial. It is geared to the alleviation of current (definable) problems rather than the promotion of desired future goals.

Incrementalism has a strong theme of normative rationality running through it – which argues that the more change takes an organization away from existing policies the higher are its unpredictable consequences, resulting in a basic strategy of maximizing security in making change. As Johnson and Scholes (1988: 25) state, 'the result is that fundamental changes in strategy in organizations

are relatively rare'. Just concentrating on managing the implementation of change may reveal incrementalism in outcomes but
says little about the incrementality (or otherwise) of the process
itself.

The assumptions of linearity in process and of rational planning
and implementation equally neglect the political and/or irrational
aspects of organization. According to Cohen *et al.* (1972), organizations are best viewed as collections of ready-made solutions
'looking for' problems. Such solutions are a product of history (what
has been done in the past in the face of similar problems) and a
product of organizational culture (normatively encouraged or
discouraged behaviour). New problems which enter the decision
arena have pre-existing and preferred solutions attached to them.
March and Olsen (1976) argue that irrationality also occurs because
preferred outcomes, the occurrence of problems and the chosen
solutions are virtually unconnected from any 'rational' perspective,
and that implementation may reflect views which have been put
forward and accepted in the organization (even though they may be
unrelated to prior discussion of the problem). Both these approaches
can be summarized as 'organized anarchy' (March and Olsen 1976).

Placing political behaviour in the frame of reference appears to
help explain the rather depoliticized accounts of anarchy by March
and Olsen (1976). The study of power and political processes in
organizations has, of course, generated a wide and varied literature.[1]
It is a field of study in its own right, yet I hope devotees of the
political models of organization will bear with me in the following
attempt to relate political perspectives of organization to the topic of
strategic change. The importance of understanding power in organizations lies in its potential for explaining how particular outcomes
were achieved, not just arguing that organizations are institutionalized collections of ready-made solutions, or that outcomes are
hampered by the cognitive and information-processing limitations
of individuals. At some risk of oversimplification, it is possible to
distinguish between three approaches to political models of organization – overt, covert and contextual. Despite their seeming mutual
exclusivity, all three are useful, since they remind us that the
outcomes of change cannot be considered independently of the
processes by which they were achieved. Furthermore, all three
approaches to power in organizations remind us that there is more
to understanding strategic change than the cognitive and information-processing aspects of organizations and individuals. Implicit in

March and Simon's (1958) work is that strategic change processes could become more linear and more 'rational' if better information technology were available. There is increasing evidence of this approach being adopted by organizations in the 1990s with the advent of data-processing, management information, executive information and decision support systems all designed to rationalize strategic change through enhancing managerial knowledge (see Martin and Clarke 1990 for a summary). The political perspective argues that, even were the knowledge base to be optimized, processes of strategic change would still be predominantly shaped, and outcomes largely determined, by the exercise of power and influence.

Overt power will be readily understood by all who work in any type of organization. The complexity of strategic tasks and the division of labour mean that localized influence attempts arise over preferred processes and outcomes. Cyert and March (1963) call this process 'local rationality' and it can arise from individuals, departments and functions as well as from organizations defending their part of a larger inter-organizational network (see Benson 1975; Evan 1971; Aldrich 1979). Theoretically developed and empirically researched by a number of scholars, the manner in which localized interests battle it out to secure their own interests in the processes of change has been well documented (see Crozier 1964; Hickson *et al.* 1971; Hinings *et al.* 1974, for example).

Covert power is the rather more invisible face of influence. Here, power is exercised through 'non-decision-making' rather than by means of influence attempts on readily identifiable (and commonly known) decision topics (Bachrach and Baratz 1970). Its exercise can take many forms, such as agenda setting, limiting participation in decisions to a select few individuals and/or defining the parameters of what is and what is not open to decision for others in the organization. The result is the same as far as the analysis of strategic change is concerned. The outcomes of change can be understood only to the extent that the characteristics of covert power are acknowledged and recognized.

Of course, non-decisions can occur in a number of ways. One lies in the literature which critically examines structural functionalism as the dominant paradigm of organization theory. The exercise of power in this case is argued to be synonymous with the structure of capitalism. As Salaman (1981: 230) argues, 'the design of work, the distribution of work rewards, the process of organizational control

and legitimation ... reflect the class relations of the wider society ...'
He goes on to argue that without this perspective 'our understanding of organizational process and structures can at best be
partial, at worst hopelessly unreal'. The outcomes of strategic
change are thus the result of manipulated and biased power plays,
firmly based in the exploitative logic of capitalism. The precise way
in which exploitation by capital and the managerial classes is
achieved is open to a number of interpretations, although organizational structure and technology would seem to be two key factors
(Burawoy 1985; Blau and Schoenherr 1971; Clegg and Dunkerley
1980; and see Scarbrough and Corbett 1992, in this series, on the
role of technology). At its most stark, organizational structure is
argued to be a tool for the domination of labour by capital; encouraging the pursuit of self-interest or sectional interest among the
managerial 'classes' and replicating societal divisions whereby class
status and position in the organizational hierarchy become compar-
able. Technology can be either a pawn or a prime mover in this
analysis. As a pawn, technology becomes the means by which
management can sustain its exploitation of labour. As a factor in its
own right, the effects of technology itself have been to deskill labour;
to relegate craft skills and individual manual dexterity to the
museum of industrial history and to cause massive reductions in
employment numbers as well as reducing future job opportunities
(see Braverman 1974; Cooley 1987).

Contextual power moves the focus of analysis towards the relations
between societal processes and structures and organizational factors.
There is more than a hint of determinism in some work at this level
of analysis (see chapter 2). In their delineation of 'radical structuralism' Burrell and Morgan (1979) argue that organizational
processes and power imbalances are largely determined by the
economic structure of society. The outcomes of strategic change are
thus not the direct result of the actions of individual managers in
individual organizations. From this analysis, if you want to explain
the 'what' of change (i.e. its outcomes), argument should focus upon
how outcomes are mediated by the deterministic forces of societal
economics. Arguments would run parallel to Marx's much cited
dictum that individuals make their own history, but not of their own
choosing. On the other hand, context could still be used to explain
the outcomes of strategic change but in a less deterministic way.
Benson (1977), for example, argues that whilst economic structures
impose a level of determinism upon individual organizational

action, there are forces and pressures for change which do emerge from individuals and organizations which either sustain or destroy societal forces. There exists a 'dialectic' between individual action and economic (or contextual) determinism.

Recent work, particularly in the field of postmodern analysis, has re-emphasized these dualities between individual or organizational action and economic and social determinism. The 'deconstruction' of knowledge bases, the hallmark of postmodern analysis, has revealed the importance of language (discourse), symbol, myth, time and timing, as well as questioning the basis of apparently plausible management recipes and solutions. Organizational changes are thus viewed as little more than the silent endorsement of preferred solutions over others. It is the outcome of change which is both the focus and the justification of its own success or failure. As Norris (1987: 162) argues, 'deconstruction is a rigorous attempt to think the limits of that principle of reason which has shaped the emergence of Western philosophy, science and technology at large'.

Examples of the potency of language in endorsing preferred solutions and world views can be found both in organizations and in wider society. Consider the following terminology used during the Gulf War of 1991.[2] ('We' refers to UN and US forces.)

We have	*They have*
Army, Navy and Air Force	A war machine
Reporting guidelines	Censorship
Press briefings	Propaganda
We	*They*
Suppress	Destroy
Eliminate	Kill
Neutralize	Kill
Decapitate	Kill
We launch	*They launch*
First strikes	Sneak missile attacks
Pre-emptively	Without provocation
Our men are	*Theirs are*
Boys, lads	Troops, hordes

So what has all this to do with organizations and change? The answer is – almost everything. To understand change fully is to view both outcomes and process as interwoven, themselves both the product and the producer of the context in which they take place. The language games above will be familiar to most managers who have been involved in organizational change. At the surface level, the 'us' and 'them' vocabulary will be familiar as protagonists and antagonists in the organization fight out the battles of change. At a deeper level, the vocabularly represents an implicit, unseen moral orthodoxy against which the success or failure of change outcomes will be valued. Deconstruction of the language of change reveals a position similar to that of 'groupthink' (Janis 1972), in which members of organizational teams and groups feel their group is 'right' and those outside it who deviate from their views are 'wrong'. The process of change thus becomes one of negotiation and persuasion between groups who assume automatically that they are in the right and reflect this both in actions and in words. Many studies have been conducted to show the intense psychological pressure placed upon individual members of a group to conform to the prevailing consensus view of the group (groupthink). Those who view the prevailing consensus as open to question are treated as troublemakers or deviants and are subjected to a range of behaviours to engender conformity (see Asch 1955; Leavitt 1972).

Symptoms of groupthink include:

1 The group feels invulnerable. There is excessive optimism and risk-taking.
2 Warnings that things might be going wrong are discounted by the group members in the name of rationality.
3 There is an unquestioned belief in the group's morality. The group will ignore questionable stances on moral or ethical issues.
4 Those who dare to oppose the group are called evil, weak or stupid.
5 There is direct pressure on anyone who opposes the prevailing mood of the group.
6 Individuals in the group self-censor if they feel that they are deviating from group norms.
7 There is an illusion of unanimity. Silence is interpreted as consent.
8 There are often self-appointed people in the group who protect it from adverse information. These people are referred to as 'mindguards'.

Janis's notion of groupthink illustrates vividly how organizations can drift towards goals which are either inappropriate or are left unquestioned. The outcomes of change are likely to be marked by the following characteristics (Wilson and Rosenfeld 1990: 150–1):

1   Information is not actively sought beyond that which is to hand, or information is only partial or biased.
2   Only a handful of alternatives are considered.
3   Those alternatives which are considered are then evaluated only partially and some are not really evaluated at all.
4   There is a strong tendency among the group members to keep things as they are and not to seek or recommend change.
5   Once an outcome is reached, there is little or no consideration of planning for any other future contingencies which might occur.

The institutionalized face of power paradoxically encourages both analysts and managers to focus predominantly on the outcomes of change and not to examine the processes by which they were achieved. Institutionalized power here refers to a blend of covert power (the taken-for-granteds and the non-decisions) and contextual power (legitimation of outcomes via language, symbol, etc.). Examples can be found in a wide range of organizational practices, some of which have been described above. Other 'sedimented' aspects of institutionalized power can be revealed through structural and cultural analyses of the organization. These are discussed in the next chapter. Two aspects which are often overlooked by authors in either the contextualist or the cultural analyses of change are gender and the sexual division of labour and the role of accounting and financial systems in shaping strategic change outcomes (and processes). Intellectual justification for dealing with these factors separately comes partly from their relative absence in what might be termed the 'general literature on organizational change' from the management writers. Second, the intellectual development of accounting practice parallels closely that of organization theory (see chapters 2 and 3). Because of this, the pervasive nature of financial systems in organizations is often overlooked, yet it too can be an important part of justifying, legitimating or inhibiting change.

GENDER: THE SEXUAL DIVISION OF LABOUR AND STRATEGIC CHANGE

Current concern with the sexual division of labour focuses very much upon equal opportunities and career development for women and men. Phrases such as the 'glass ceiling', which describes how women can progress to senior positions in organizations yet fail consistently to be appointed to the top jobs, are much in vogue. So, too, are demographic predictions, which show that we are soon to approach an era where organizations will be forced to cater for a labour force proportionately more female than ever before and that traditional sexual attitudes and stereotypes will have to be explicitly addressed and broken down. Whether or not such demographic predictions are accurate, the sexual division of labour has a long history in the story of organizational change. So much so, that analyses of the impact of organizational change upon the individual almost invariably need untangling by gender. How one views, accepts, struggles against or promotes organizational change will depend to a great extent on whether one is a woman or a man. Equally, homosexuality and lesbianism are subject to their own set of discriminatory organizational practices, mostly aimed at suppression. Most business organizations do not advertise any 'gay' areas in their labour force. It is something to be covered up or ignored. The prevailing current against change in these cases seems to be preservation of the *status quo*. Organizational staff are to remain heterosexual.

To cover the field of gender with any sense of intellectual justice or completeness would need more than a book in itself. Here some key issues which focus directly upon strategic change are highlighted. If some form of intellectual defence for this somewhat artificial separation of a large sociological debate is required, it is that at least this analysis recognizes the role of gender (however partially) and views questions of gender as key factors in the analysis of strategic change. Many avoid or ignore the issue altogether, assuming a relatively neutral, male-dominated, heterosexual organizational context.

Corporate strategy appears at best a sexually neutral world, at worst a virtually all-male world of managerial and executive action. Indeed, female leaders of organizations or of strategic change are usually singled out for special media attention, such is their rarity. An obvious example is Anita Roddick, who founded the Body Shop in 1976 on a budget of £4,000 and with fifteen products in bottles with hand-written labels. Today, there are in excess of 300 products sold through some 340 shops (some company-owned, the majority franchises). In 1985 she was proclaimed Businesswoman of the Year, in 1988 was Communicator of the Year, and she recently received the OBE. Anita Roddick has featured consistently in both the general media and the business press as something of a phenomenon, not least because of her gender.

Another example can be found not in business but in international government. At the end of 1990 Professor Sadako Ogata became the female High Commissioner for Refugees for the United Nations. A self-declared international organization founded on principles of egalitarianism, the United Nations has a sorry record as far as women are concerned. A woman has never held the job of Secretary General (the most senior position). Furthermore, there has never been a woman candidate for the post. Of the remaining executive positions, only two have been held by women (and around 140 men have been appointed) since the end of the Second World War. Even the United Nations Charter refers to the Secretary General as unquestionably male, referring to the 'entrustment' of the organization to 'him' (Article 98). Today women represent four countries to the United Nations. One hundred and fifty-five representatives are men.

Among other areas, the relatively poor representation (and hence inability to influence the outcome of strategic change) of women in senior positions can be found in many of the professions as well as in the boardrooms of business. In a recent report (Department of Health 1988) it was pointed out that whilst half of medical school students were women, only 15 per cent held positions as consultants; only 3 per cent of consultant surgeons were women and less than 1 per cent were general surgeons (eleven women in England and Wales from a total of 1,217 positions). Recently government initiatives have been launched to overcome obstacles to women (overt and covert), and among them the allocation of £1.5 million to help swell the numbers of part-time posts for women as registrars and an initiative to avoid discrimination in appointment procedures.

Of course, such examples are only the visible tip of the iceberg. It is easy to gather data showing the extremely low levels of representation of women in senior positions both in public-sector and private organizations. Lack of representation will necessarily reduce the influence of women in decisions concerning strategic change. More covert is the implication that a lack of change (preservation of the *status quo*) may be a function of witting or unwitting male decisions. The factors which have encouraged gender imbalances and the exclusion of women from decision-making may be summarized as:

1   *Family and education.* Subordination of the woman's role through the preservation of the patriarchal family. Women are totally responsible for child care and for supporting the family whilst the male joins the labour market. The perpetuation of this differentiation is reflected in schooling and education generally (e.g. role stereotyping).
2   *Dual labour market.* Women occupy a secondary role in the labour market. Their labour is viewed as 'optional'. Employment is often on different terms from men's, with women receiving different wages and conditions of employment.
3   *Organizational structure.* Preserves the position of elites in society (i.e. men) by replicating societal structure in organizations. Men are thus able to protect their political and vested interests.
4   *Organizational processes.* Strategic change is a process of dealing with uncertainty. One area in which men can reduce uncertainty is by sticking to what they know and can control (e.g. the employment of men in senior positions).
5   *National cultures/and ideologies.* Dominant expectations about the appropriateness of gender roles, e.g. males are to be active leaders and 'need' full-time employment. Females are to be passive home-makers and do not really need primary employment (this extreme is particularly evident in western industrialized societies).

    The notion of the family as a necessary adjunct to capitalism has afforded it primacy of place in ensuring that complex organizations are male-dominated (Gardiner 1976). Males work in the labour market whilst women provide the labour of being wives and mothers inside the family. This arrangement allows males the time (and energy) to participate in full-time work. Equally, this societal model is often uncritically accepted throughout the education system, with traditional male–female roles replicated especially at the primary and secondary school levels (Shaw 1976). The dual labour market is a concept in which women are argued to form the secondary source of labour and in which men are the primary source (see Barker and Allen 1976). Important consequences of this analysis are that disparities occur in payment levels between primary and secondary labour markets, with the latter being relatively poorly paid (sometimes for the same job). Little career transition or progression is possible between the two labour markets, and the primary market is characterized by structured career routes and opportunities. The secondary labour market has virtually no career structure, employment being seen as something of a luxury for those who wish to earn a bit more income, feeling at the same time a little guilty about the opportunity cost of not being able to look after the family full-time. Even where males and females work together doing the same job, differentials other than pay disparity exist. Walsh, (1989: 112), for example, shows how in a British textile mill the transformation from a previously female-dominated labour force to one which was predominantly male (during the 1960s) was argued to be justified, since the advent of shift working was held to be inappropriate for woman because of their 'domestic responsibilities'. She also shows how further technical changes involved in textile manufacture systematically favoured male employees, since they were 'less adversely affected by technical changes'.

Organizational structures and processes, the very foundations of organizational change, are again apparently male-biased. To talk of change is predominantly to talk the language of a single sex. Kanter (1977) argues that the exclusion of women from the seats of organizational power is largely due to a desire on the part of males to maintain the *status quo* and to retain security and certainty in the uncertain world of strategic decision-making. Because strategic decisions are uncertain and their trajectory is full of discontinuity and interrupts (see Hickson *et al.* 1986), male executives create a niche of security by working with other males and selecting junior executives from the male ranks to continue the tradition. By selecting what they know they preserve at least one element of certainty. The gender arguments for organizational structure are ones we have visited earlier in this chapter – namely that organizational structure reflects the elitist elements of the wider society of which it is a part. Taking this politicized view of organization, Offe (1976) argues that discrimination against women occurs because of the tendency for (male) elites to maintain the *status quo* by rewarding and advancing those most like themselves. In this way, it is argued, the common interest is preserved. Finally, the arguments at the societal level of analysis suggest that changes here are also likely to be male-biased, since differential expectations are built into the societal system. At least in western industrial societies, males expect relative independence and full-time employment away from the home and are encouraged in their view of women primarily as managers of the home (Wolff 1977).

These points raise serious questions about change in organizations, for it depends very much upon one's perception of organization whether or not gender enters the debate. Mills (1988) identifies the extremes of the positions taken towards gender. On the one hand, much organizational analysis views firms as gender-free places in the sense that males and females are treated alike. (The Hawthorne studies are a good example of this, as was much of scientific management; so too, are many studies which explicitly examine organizational culture.) On the other hand, an analysis which distinguishes gender as a central factor in creating and sustaining organizational processes will start from the position that gender is central to 'the development of internal organizational dynamics' (Hearn and Parkin 1983: 228).

Burrell (1984) takes the gender debates further by suggesting that powerful forces for preserving the *status quo* or for justifying change can best be understood in terms of sexuality rather than gender difference. Accepting that much organizational analysis has marginalized or ignored gender, Burrell argues that relationships between or within the genders (hetero- and homosexuality) hold the key to understanding power, control and resistance to change. As Burrell (1984: 99) says, 'the complete eradication of sexuality from bureaucratic structures has been a goal which many top decision makers have pursued'. In other words, formal organizations become desexualized, leaving sexual relationships to time and space outside formal working hours. The problem, of course, with this is that it ignores the permeability (both subjective and objective) of 'social' life and 'organizational' life. Issues of discrimination, the commodification of women for men's pleasure and power inequalities are as evident within the organization as they are in wider society. Pollert (1981) shows the potency of this interrelationship between societal values and organizational practice. Describing how employment rules specify that women are not to be employed in certain types of work (e.g. heavy physical jobs), she graphically illustrates how 'local' pressure in the area surrounding a textile mill supported the role of women in being assigned physically heavy and demanding work. It was the 'expected' role of women, irrespective of national legislation which advised to the contrary.

Finally, image, language and symbolic behaviour in organizations (again the very stuff of organizational culture) have an impact upon the question of gender in organizational change. For women who do break through the glass ceiling, the decisions they make are far more open to questioning of their judgement by male staff than if the decisions had been made by a man. Rosen and Jerdee (1974) show this in a study of supervisors; Brorverman (1972) shows that even when women adopt roles and exhibit behaviour normatively encouraged in male managers, their behaviour is viewed as suspicious and open to question. Organizational language, such as that of leadership and of team-building, is often couched in both male and militaristic language. Leaders are naturally assumed to be male and to be aggressive role models for other males to follow (Riley 1983). Less well studied, and with no systematic empirical examples known to the author, are the ambivalent attitudes adopted towards female and male organizational leaders in wider society. Male leaders who become widely known through the media often 'suffer' investigations into their sexual activities, especially in the tabloid press. Revelations of extra-marital affairs are relatively common. Yet for the male executive these are not necessarily viewed as cause for moral outrage or perhaps removal from office. Often, the reverse seems the case. Sexual adventures are described in language which amplifies a macho and aggressively successful image. Conquests in the sexual arena seem to imply a similar ability to achieve business conquests and deals in the boardroom. For the few women who occupy such senior positions, such media revelations would be unlikely to take the same perspective or allow the same ambivalence between organizational and social life.

THE ROLE OF ACCOUNTING AND FINANCIAL SYSTEMS

It is remarkable how many texts in the field of organizational change not only emphasize the outcomes of change but also concentrate almost exclusively upon the behavioural aspects of achieving those ends. Very few scholars have chosen to concentrate their studies upon the impact of the more quantitative aspects of management accounting upon organizational change. Yet the field of accounting itself is beginning to develop a critical edge, much of which reveals the institutionalized potency of financial systems for shaping strategic change. Much of the debate, which tends to be restricted to academics in the financial disciplines, has direct relevance to understanding both the outcomes and the processes of change (see, for example, Hopwood 1978, 1983; Burchell *et al.* 1980; Otley 1984).

The basic thesis underlying the critique in accounting theory and practice is that both financial theory and practice are shaped by and shape the organizational context in which they operate. Accounting theories may appear to be objective, aimed at providing information and guidelines for decision-making, yet they are also a pervasive force in shaping organizational change. Whilst organization theory was charting its course from scientific management to postmodern concerns, so too the theories of accounting were beginning to become reflexive. It is possible to see a number of similarities between the development of knowledge in both fields, organization theory and accounting, and to show how the one supports, guides and sustains the other.

Based on the neoclassical theory of the firm, early accounting theories were derived direct from cost accounting practice. The main aim of such quantitative practice was to control production and to monitor/reduce factory costs. Immediate parallels can be drawn here between cost accounting and scientific management. The organization is viewed in terms of its costs, which, like bricklaying or manufacturing, can be managed toward greater efficiency. The assumptions both of accounting and of organization theory are of rational individuals operating in a closed, rational system of organization. Management accounting was thus a means of effecting organizational change through providing seemingly unambiguous data which could guide managers towards making greater savings and rationalizing efficiency. Financial data were routinely generated (a natural part of organizational life), were easily quantifiable (and thus tangible, unlike human behaviour), were a unidimensional measure of organizational performance, providing a powerful set of arguments for organizational change (divisions and departments could be monitored financially and their viability could be questioned).

Just as in organization theory, management accounting progressed from this apparent certainty and rationality towards models and theories which allowed uncertainty, ambiguity and human behaviour to be included. Consideration of uncertainty led down one path towards contingency models of management accounting, information economics, game theory and transaction cost analysis (see Jaedicke and Robichek 1964; Demski 1972; Otley 1980; Roberts and Scapens 1985). Consideration of human behaviour led down another path towards management accounting theories accommodating the interplay between individuals and accounting systems, especially looking at the influence of individuals and groups on the design of accounting systems (see Lowe and Shaw 1968; Schiff and Lewin 1970; Burchell *et al.* 1980).

The importance of these developments for understanding organizational change lies in a number of areas. First, management accounting originally developed in relative isolation from complex organizations. It was the product of academia and professional institutes. Placing management accounting in the context of economic organization paved the way for accounting being both the engine of change and its rationalization. Meyer and Rowan (1977), for example, argue that, whilst management accounting is usually seen as a rather neutral, technical aspect of organization, it can easily be employed in a symbolic rather than a purely technical sense. The myth and ceremony of organizational life are bolstered by often complex financial systems which are themselves geared more to achieving symbolic ends than to sustaining the purely economic activity of organization. Following the same theme, Pettigrew (1985) argues that, far from being neutral information, management accounting provides a very convenient source of interpretive meaning for individuals (including *post hoc* rationalization of decisions already taken). Managers can attribute a variety of meanings to accounts and financial systems, according to their disposition. Depending upon the desired outcome of change, managers can interpret and reinterpret their rationales, using management accounting as a political device. On the same theme, Wildavsky (1979) shows that the overall analysis of organizational 'intelligence' requires budgeting, financial planning and accounting systems to be viewed as inextricably interwoven with organizational politics and power games. Those political interests which can seek to sway the outcome of decisions by the exercise of power will often use financial 'data' to support their cause or to refute the countervailing claims of others (see Hickson *et al.*, 1986).

A further consistent theme, particularly in the mainstream literature of accounting, has been that of optimism. Increasingly sensitive and sophisticated accounting systems were going to make things better, through reforming what was already in place, exercising financial control where none previously existed, or by a steady process of constant improvement. Change bolstered by new or improved financial systems was always going to be for the better.

Recent work in the disciplines of finance and accounting[3] questions both the role of and the optimism inherent in accounting practice.

Summarizing the main themes of this theoretical work, the role of accounting in organizational change comprises:

1   An increasing pressure upon managers and organizations to foreshorten time horizons. This puts immense pressure to reduce or depress investment in intangibles such as research and development or new product development.

2   Some business sectors suffer more from this pressure than others. Pharmaceutical organizations in the UK, for example, manage relatively high levels of R&D and new product investment. Conversely, mechanical engineering concerns and vehicle manufacturers are typical examples in the UK where accounting pressures have helped to suppress innovation (see Whipp and Clark 1986; Tailby and Whitston 1989).

3   Middle managers face constraints on their decision-making autonomy through management accounting performance measures. The need to demonstrate tangible performance in the short term, often coupled with relatively short career spans in any one organization, leads to managers becoming selfish about what they promote in organizations. A reinforcement of local rationality takes place (Cyert and March 1963).

4   Senior managers are constrained in a different way. Auditing measures of performance set powerful boundaries around strategic action. Stock market evaluation is directly affected by auditing performance measures, and many senior managers find themselves defending the organization against take-over threats as a result of 'poor' evaluation. If change requires investment in new capital, then auditing measures of performance will again be a major influence, since it is cheaper to raise equity capital in 'better'-performing organizations than in 'average' or 'poorer' performers.

SUMMARY

The focus solely on outcomes, therefore, would seem untenable in the study of strategic change. Yet this is belied by the weight of literature which adopts the goal-directed model of a preconceived vision. Some of the processes which shape and fashion the direction and nature of change have been outlined in this chapter. The focus has been upon the institutionalized weight of vested interests, the importance of context and the hidden rules of the game which lend an air of rationality to decision-making. (Gender and financial systems were selected for special attention, given their relative neglect in much of the literature.) However, the chapter also began by emphasizing the analytical complexities in assuming too neat a distinction between process and outcome. Nowhere is the blurring between the two more pronounced than in the studies which have sprung from the cultural and structural approaches to organizations. These are explored in the next chapter.

Chapter 5

Organizational culture and change

No account of strategic change could avoid some consideration of the role of corporate culture, such has been its pervasiveness in management theory and practice towards organizational change. 'Change the culture and the majority of current organizational problems will be solved' has become something of a recurrent theme from many students of management, theorists and consultants alike. The phrase (like the term 'culture') is a useful catch-all, incorporating broad aspects of organization, including control, commitment, socialization, manipulation (looking at groups and individuals) and structure, design and corporate performance (at the organizational level of analysis). Despite a growing empirical research base which testifies to the difficulty in defining, let alone managing, organizational culture (see Pettigrew 1990c; Pettigrew and Whipp 1991), it has remained a seductive concept, imbued with a seemingly elixir-like quality for facilitating corporate change and renewal.

No definitions of organizational culture are given here. The primary reason for this lies partly in the difficulty of precision (since culture appears to include virtually everything in an organization, any definition must do the same) and partly in being unable to resolve the inherent differences which abound in current definitions in the literature. Such incompatability lies along a number of dimensions, including tangibility–intangibility (culture is viewed as something which is directly manageable, or as something much deeper and more symbolic); or culture is viewed variously as an analytical construct or as an applicable variable (culture can only be understood in terms of symbols, subjective meaning, language and context, or is a set of identifiable factors which can be managed directly towards a given end). This chapter will examine a number of theoretical and empirical approaches, each of which has arisen and been developed under the banner of organizational culture, in an attempt to lead to a critical evaluation of the concept as it relates to organizational change.

First, it is necessary to locate the concept of culture within some overall framework to see how it fits in relation to other theories of organization (some of which have already been covered in the previous chapters). This is no easy task. The distinction between the applicable and the analytical approaches to organizational culture has been outlined by Wilson and Rosenfeld (1990). Yet this only illuminates one facet of the concept and primarily distinguishes between the different uses to which organizational culture is put. It does not locate the concept in sociological space. However, in a prize-winning analysis, Risto (1990) provides a framework within which it is possible to locate the main cultural approaches to organizations (see fig. 5). Placing organizational culture in the context of three distinguishable approaches to the sociology of organizations (the structure of social action, symbols and codes of meaning and theories of social action) allows different approaches to culture to be analytically separated as well as considered at different levels of analysis.

The major distinction in fig. 5 is that between structural and interpretive views of culture. Interpretive views hold organizational culture to be something created through symbols, language and ritual. The language used to describe organizational events, the symbols commonly employed to denote status and membership, and the way in which individuals act out their various roles, create and maintain the cultural fabric of the organization. Goffman (1982) offers a number of illustrations drawn from the everyday behaviour of people both at work and in social life. Looking first at individuals, he argues that the dramaturgical metaphor is useful in describing the type of behaviour observed. That is, individuals act out a part within the context of a wider organization. They can write the parts themselves, or can act them out within some preformed or prescribed role, very much in the manner of a stage actor. Mangham (1986) has directly applied this kind of dramatic role analysis to the behaviour of individual managers during the course of a decision-making process. For both authors, two factors are key – the performance itself and the individual's belief in his or her performance.

More structural analyses rely more upon how roles are structured together to form particular organizational designs. The shape or

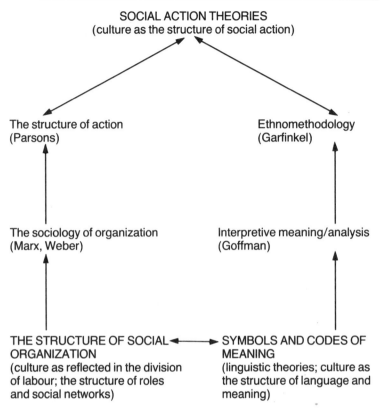

SOCIAL ACTION THEORIES
(culture as the structure of social action)

The structure of action
(Parsons)

Ethnomethodology
(Garfinkel)

The sociology of organization
(Marx, Weber)

Interpretive meaning/analysis
(Goffman)

THE STRUCTURE OF SOCIAL ◄──────► SYMBOLS AND CODES OF
ORGANIZATION   MEANING
(culture as reflected in the division   (linguistic theories; culture as
of labour; the structure of roles   the structure of language and
and social networks)   meaning)

Figure 5.1 Organizational culture in the context of the sociology of
organizations (adapted from Risto 1990)

configuration of an organization becomes an important facet of its
culture. Handy's (1986) widely known distinction between four
typologies of organizational culture represents a specific attempt to
describe the division of labour, the structure of roles and social
networks. Indeed, the cultures themselves are described primarily
by organizational structures. Power cultures are those which are
centrally controlled by a single individual or group. This power
centre determines the culture, since the structure of the organization
(a spider's web) allows the all-powerful spider to control key organization processes (such as decision-making) in whatever way is
deemed suitable. Similarly, bureaucratic structures are characterized by role cultures in which processes are subject to rule, prece-
dent and regulation. Matrix structures allow the culture of the task

or the business project to become the dominant philosophy of the organization and, finally, almost structureless organizations (clusters) allow a culture of professional independence to be maintained (see Handy, 1986, for a full description of the culture/structure analysis).

Both the interpretive and the structural views of organizational culture lead towards very different interpretations of the process of organizational change. As has been the case throughout the history of organization theory, the structuralists have emerged with a greater volume of empirical research at their disposal (compared with interpretivists), often coupled with an overriding normative conviction that certain cultures and structures supported organizational change whilst others hindered or detracted from its realization. Perhaps the most famous (or infamous) of these approaches over the last decade has been the 'tradition' of achieving organizational 'excellence' through the management of organizational culture. This is examined in the next section.

THE STRUCTURE OF CULTURE: 'IT ALL COMES FROM PEOPLE'

So said Tom Peters in the introduction to the film of the book *In Search of Excellence* (Peters and Waterman 1982). Prior to this discovery (paraphrasing Peter's introduction) we made the awful mistake of equating corporate success with organizational structures (such as bureaucracies) when instead what really mattered was having an organizational culture which placed people first on the managerial agenda. Such a culture required almost fanatical devotion from individuals to the organization, but for its part the organization was designed around these devotees, with lean management structures, clear communication lines and responsible autonomy right down the line. Bureaucracies were 'out'. Task-centred, decentralized, human-based organizations were 'in', since they could facilitate and sustain organizational change (and, in turn, contribute to sustained organizational performance). These were the 'excellent' organizations. Perhaps unsurprisingly, these organizations, drawn from a number of mostly North American samples, conformed in many respects to the tenets of traditional management theory, and, to be fair, Peters and Waterman never made any claim to originality. Yet the excellence tradition (which followed the publication of Peters and Waterman's book in 1982) was to fuel the fires of corporate culture in a way unprecedented in management theory and practice. A whole variety of organizations became engaged in contortions of change, trying to emulate 3M, Disney, McDonald's and the other examples of excellence. A whole consultancy industry also apparently sprang up overnight to help them achieve it.

Organizational culture and organizational change became close bedfellows, since the one was thought to be inextricably linked with the other. The causal arguments for this link are cast in a linear fashion and are unidirectional. First, culture and organizational performance are argued to be inextricably linked. Second, to achieve changes in organizational performance, manipulation of the organizational culture by attention to its structure are the first factors for attention. Third, decentralized, project-based organizations which place individuals at the centre of organizational attention are those which succeed. Such emphases are restricted neither to American reorganizations nor to those in the private sector. Fig. 6, taken from a national newspaper in England, is advertising for someone to create and lead precisely this kind of culture. The organization is from the public sector in the heart of Yorkshire, where the term 'culture' (used in the advert) has traditionally applied more to beer, cricket and other county matters than to creating excellent organizations. Note that the term 'culture change' appears in the advert without further explanation, as if everybody knows what it means, and is agreed on the concept of organizational culture.

Intellectual justification for the excellence approach is surprisingly hard to find, given its near universality in organization theory. It falls down at the early hurdles of both empirical and theoretical enquiry. Below are summarized the major criticisms that have been levelled at the concept of achieving change towards a model of excellence.

Empirical issues:

1   The failure of many excellent companies to sustain corporate success.
2   The availability of alternative explanations of success (such as monopoly position in the market).
3   Mostly poor sampling among the studies, so that it is not known how far the organizations are representative.
4   The virtual omission of key business sectors, such as petrochemicals, motor manufacturing, financial services, etc.

Figure 5.2 Culture change in Yorkshire: a difficult but well paid task?
(*The Guardian*, 5 March 1991)

Theoretical issues:

1   Assumes a 'one best way' of organizing.
2   Assumes a simple causal relationship between culture and performance.
3   Generally dominated by a top-management view of the organization.
4   Lacks a well argued theoretical basis, preferring to borrow selectively from other work.

There is no doubting the emphasis on people as agents of organizational change in the excellence tradition. The question is whether organizational culture and excellent performance consist of anything more than the ceremonious, the ritual and the symbolic, aimed at securing emotional attachment to the organization (Peters and Waterman 1982). The evidence to date suggests that there is indeed much more.

Approximately two years following the publication of *In Search of Excellence* some twenty of the original sample firms studied as models of excellence in the face of change were experiencing severe problems. All had achieved the outcomes of management through people, of 'sticking to the knitting' and of keeping management levels lean and simple. Yet the experience of these organizations questioned the central tenets of excellence. For example, Walt Disney was to produce a continued string of failures in films, Caterpillar experienced declining demand for its heavy plant machinery and Atari, the name once synonymous with computer games, almost disappeared entirely. Indeed, Disney's most successful film after a string of relative failures (*Splash*) was one which did not go through the usual procedures of the film review board identified as a key to success by Peters and Waterman.

The example of Atari epitomizes many of the dangers in assuming that successful outcomes in the recent past (outcomes) can inform the formulation of tomorrow's strategies (processes). By 'sticking to the knitting' Atari effectively dominated the video-game market worldwide in 1981. As Tasini (1991: 68) notes, the organization amassed $323 million in earnings during 1982 under the banner of its parent company (Warner Communications). By 1983 Atari had lost $539 million. The company still had a culture of productivity through people, yet its product strategy was awry. Atari had precious few other products with which it could offset the massive losses. In 1984 the company was sold to Jack Tramiel (the founder of Commodore International) and the organization began to revive. Today, however, Atari has only around a 5 per cent share of the market.

The example of Atari allows us to attribute causes other than organizational culture to both success and failure. The video-game market exploded in 1981 and never ceased in its insatiable demand on producers for something new. Innovation capacity was at a premium, but so too was diversification. Organizations needed a range of products to survive in the market. Furthermore, the pace of change in this market far outstripped any organization's ability to change its culture. Alternative explanations of organizational performance can be found elsewhere among the ranks of the 'excellent'. For example, Delamarter's (1988) analysis of IBM's success differs markedly from that of Peters and Waterman.

According to Peters and Waterman, IBM's success is directly attributable to sustaining innovation and the desire to change by deliberately manipulating the culture of the organization so that deviants and heretics are structured into teams and project groups controlled by a strong central management philosophy. Delamarter's interpretation of IBM's success lies largely in its monopoly position in the market rather than in any managerial style or organizational culture. Similarly, Silver (1987) accounts for organizational performance in very different ways from Peters and Waterman. He interprets McDonalds' corporate culture as one of scientific management, wherein deskilled and monotonous jobs are the rule, bolstered by a ready supply of cheap young labour.

In other significant empirical studies of organizational culture the links between economic performance and culture remain inconclusive. Denison's (1984, 1990) study of thirty-four firms was drawn from a sample of 43,747 individual respondents represented by 6,671 groups. The data indicate that return on investment and return on sales appear to be positively related to decentralized, participative decision-making processes, especially where they are a consistent aspect of organizational culture. Thus we might conclude that managing cultural change towards this end would be worth while in the pursuit of better economic performance. But, before long, Denison reveals that consistent cultures based upon participative decision-making also appear to have a strong relationship with below-average long-term performance. We are caught between the devil and the deep blue sea. Denison's extensive data set raises even more questions about the concept of organizational culture as measured by organizational climate, work design, leadership styles and group processes. Managing cultural change may result in short-term economic benefits, but in the longer term may result in stagnation and eventually seal the economic demise of the organization.

Both Schein (1984) and Meyer and Zucker (1989) make similar points regarding organizations which fail. Whilst the usual correlation between 'strong' organizational cultures and organizational performances pervades much of the literature, Meyer and Zucker show that a key factor is precisely the type or the nature of the strong culture. For example, some 'strong' cultures such as owner-managed organizations displayed a greater tendency to fail than 'strong' cultures which were professionally managed, with ownership separated from control. The basic keystone variable in Meyer and Zucker's analysis of culture lies in the motivation of individual managers to keep the organization going in the face of hardship or decline. Of course, the literature is full of different definitions of organizational performance and organizational decline, but Meyer and Zucker's analysis should give pause for thought on the part of those analysts who assume a linear and causal argument between cultural change and organizational performance.

In a rare European empirical study of organizational culture, Calori and Sarnin (1991) examined five French firms all engaged in only one line of business. Their definition of culture was drawn from a list of ninety-six 'values' (often explicitly written down in French organizations) and from ninety-two management practices gathered by means of a questionnaire. Each organization in the sample was following a strategy of differentiation and operated in a mature industry. Again, the findings were mixed. Strength, or homogeneity of culture, appeared to be related to sustained economic growth. Yet profitability was not significantly related to organizational culture. As the authors say, 'very few values and corresponding management practices seem to be associated with profitability' (Calori and Sarnin 1991: 68).

It is likely that other factors are at play in the culture–performance arguments. Not least is the implication from the above studies that organizational culture can serve initially as a useful device for establishing core values such as team spirit, collective responsibility, consistency and quality. These can help to provide the energy for organizational growth. Yet, in time, they can also stifle profitability, since the organization gets locked into specific ways of operating and the new-found strong culture increases the levels of resistance to changing it. This is the paradox of organizational slack.

Organizational slack is where 'organizations ... can satisfy their explicit objectives with less than a complete expenditure of organizational "energy"' (March and Simon 1958: 126). If an organization is effective, then *ceteris paribus* it will inevitably create slack. On the one hand increased levels of slack make it easier to implement organizational change, since the slack acts as a cushion against the immediacy of drastic changes. Yet it simultaneously lowers the motivation of individuals to undertake the change, largely because they are happy as they are. Thus slack can, in time, alter the sensitivity of an organization in recognizing problems and in responding to environmental changes (Hedberg 1981).

LOOKING FOR CLUES: INTERPRETIVE VIEWS OF CULTURE

Following an interpretive view of culture leads us to a very different analytical and methodological perspective on how sense may be made of organizational change. Instead of looking for clues in the structural and strategic patterns of organizations, an interpretive view requires that change is analysed from the perspective of the individual's definition of the situation as he or she interprets it. It is no longer sufficient to account for change as a sequence of processes sustained by a friendly and supportive organizational culture. What fundamentally matters are the cognitive and interpretive processes by which individuals either support change, facilitate it for others, or seek to destroy it. Thus interpretation, symbols and language lie at the heart of this view.

At first sight it may appear that the interpretive view is more obscure, less readily analysable than the structural perspectives. This is not inevitably the case. Evidence of the potency of symbols, for example, can be found in almost every organization, from individual dress 'codes' to corporate logos. Just as individuals seek medical advice, organizations can now consult professionals about their identity (its meaning, or lack of it, perhaps). Corporate identity 'doctors' such as Wolff Olins have come to the fore in recent years, as exemplified not least by the controversy over British Telecom's new corporate logo (designed in consultation with Wolff Olins). Both public and trade unions were unhappy not only about the logo itself (what did it signify, and what was wrong with the old one?) but also about the cost (an estimated £50 million) of changing the logo on some 40,000 vehicles, 70,000 uniforms and almost 100,000 telephone boxes. Symbols, evidently, do not come cheap. Yet they are potent. Despite British Telecom's radical 'downsizing', shedding almost 11,000 jobs in 1990–91, with more losses to come, the unions appear convinced that the new symbol is worth while, lending their support to the change of image depicting BT as a truly global player in the communications industry. At least for the time being, it seems, the corporate mission and its symbolic hoopla placed the pervasive issues of industrial relations change very much in the background. Thus symbolism takes primacy in the context of change rather than the issues of labour relations, organizational structure and strategic decision-making.

Lest the reader think this perhaps too cynical a view of organizational change, consider the ways in which the potent forces of corporate symbolism are also bolstered by language (see Mitroff and Kilmann 1976: Pettigrew 1979). Only ten or so years ago the literature on change management was using a vocabulary which seems very different from that of today. Although concerned expressly with organizational change, the work of Lewin and other researchers who focused on the social psychology of organization was primarily oriented towards examining the relevance of theories to organizational practice. As such, their role was that of the traditional researcher, taking concepts such as small group behaviour and seeing to what extent it helped explain what was going on in any particular organizational change. Today the role of the traditional researcher has arguably been usurped by the wordsmith, in particular by the wordsmith who has mastery of the pithy phrase and who can fashion a colourful metaphor. In a remarkably short time the language used by practising managers, by many management trainers and by many researchers has coalesced into a diorama of metaphor (and no, that's not an example). Virtually everything that moves within an organization is subject to metaphor:

1   Organizations are no longer described by what they produce or do; they have mission statements instead.

2   Mission statements are meant to 'cascade down' the organization and are the means of individual 'empowerment'.

3   This empowerment in turn leads to great teams who run hot, who play passionately (even chaotically), towards the corporate mission, united in their common vision.

4   Organizations are no longer run by managers but by heroes

who are insanely great in what they do. They turn threats into opportunities, presumably by constantly gazing through that double-glazed window of opportunity towards the distant horizons of total quality.

This is not to say that metaphor is not a useful device. It is, in moderation. Yet how many of those individuals who are supposed to inform each other through research (managers, organization theorists, etc.) find themselves instead swapping metaphors of some assumed reality? Less charitable authors have termed the vocabulary of dominant metaphor 'MBA-speak' (Burrell 1991: 145).

The potency of symbol and language is, of course, an area of academic study in its own right. We can do no more than alert the reader here to the dangers of employing metaphor as a substitute for knowledge and as a shorthand device for describing an assumed consensus. As an example, consider the currently fashionable notion of the 'intrapreneur' – the often cited internal change agent. Most texts seem to agree on the broad characteristics of anyone in this role, although even here strong research evidence is hard to come by. Intrapreneurs have an eye for opportunities; they initiate action rather than respond to circumstances; they are restless, active and persistent, and will often rely on persuasion, encouragement, even guile if it gets results. Yet anyone displaying these characteristics in late medieval Britain would have been termed a devil. Such actions were anti-God and against God's dignity. By the end of the fourteenth century, such characteristics were those of the satirist, the individual who could question the system. By late Jacobean times the characteristics described the gallant, the individual who fought against all odds to achieve his goals, often subverting the law to do so. Yet all is forgiven in the end. Readers of Victorian romantic novels will recognize the gallant hero. In more modern times such characteristics have been incorporated into industrial organization to describe entrepreneurial activity in general.[1]

These views and criticisms are rooted in ethnomethodological studies of organization (where individuals' definitions of the situation are given pre-eminence over other methods of data collection, especially survey or cross-sectional data gathering). However, there is a relative dearth of interpretive empirical evidence, in comparison to the more structuralist interpretations of organizational change. In particular areas of human activity (rather than strictly in complex organizations) the interpretive approach has been well researched.

Deaths, hospitals, suicides, police activity in dealing with down-and-outs, dental practice and gynaecological clinics have all been focuses of study (see Sudnow 1967, Garfinkel 1967, for example). In each case the definition of the situation of the participant is taken to explain the phenomena of change. For example, a woman would be unlikely to define the situation she encounters in a gynaecological clinic as pre-dominantly sexual, yet in many other contexts such would undoubtedly be the case. The ability of the gynaecologist to act unhindered depends largely upon the woman's changed definition of the situation upon entering the clinic. Interpretive studies of change in complex business organizations are relatively rare.

Silverman (1970) made a general plea for understanding organizational phenomena (including change) from the commonsense perspective of the individual. Clegg (1975) empirically studied this perspective, concluding that power, influence and deeply rooted rules in organizations were best uncovered by examining individuals' accounts. During the 1980s it seemed that the structuralists dominated virtually all aspects of strategic change, although there are notable exceptions such as Pettigrew's (1985) analysis of change in ICI, where he blends individual accounts from managers with more macro-contextual factors. Hickson et al.'s (1986) study of strategic decision-making processes similarly blended the narratives of individual managers with more 'objective' criteria of process characteristics (such as the duration or continuity/discontinuity of a decision process).

By the late 1980s and early 1990s, however, researchers were beginning to link interpretation and organizational change explicitly. Isabella (1990), for example, argues that to understand organizational change fully requires more than just analysing the sequence of process. Individual cognition and interpretation are the key to understanding change. Like Quinn and Kimberly (1984: 303), Isabella views organizational transition as itself subject to change. Therefore interpretation is vital, since acceptance of any change confirms what was previously novel and ultimately turns innovation into routine.

Isabella (1990) studied forty managers from medium-size financial service organizations, all of which were undergoing substantial changes both internally and externally. She searched managers' narratives for themes or similarities (validating this technique by using others not involved with the project to code the data; they produced identical themes). Four key stages of interpretation were identified (adapted from Isabella 1990: 7–41):

1   *Anticipation.* Rumours, the grape vine, news and general news present a puzzle to individuals in the organization. Reality is created by each individual as he or she tries to connect pieces of information together. Depending upon the ways in which such connections are made, different pictures of anticipation of future changes emerge.

2   *Confirmation.* This is the stage at which anticipation is confirmed. There is, however, little objective reality. The jigsaw of interpretation involves piecing together fragments of information into a stereotypical or conventional frame of reference. In many ways this is reminiscent of incrementalism, since stereotypes and frames of reference are often formed from what has happened in the past. These are subsequently used to inform and guide future action.

3   *Culmination.* This is the stage at which an individual will amend his or her prior interpretation of an event. These amendments are no longer standard frames of reference (as in 2 above) but reconstructions of what has happened. This is organizational history in the making. Closely linked into organizational symbolism, this process involves individuals looking for clues from which to derive new meanings (or to reconfirm existing interpretations of events).

4   *Aftermath.* The final stage, during which events (the change) are tested and subjected to experimentation. This is to confirm the construed reality, and in the process, the winners and losers of the change process become easily identifiable.

This interpretive approach anchors the notion of corporate culture into a personalization. What will the changes mean for me? In order to answer the question, individuals make sense of the information they have and piece it together within the context of current and past organizational events. Predictions can also be made, therefore, by individuals about how they will fare in the future scenario. They can then decide whether or not to see the change through, or perhaps look for alternatives within the same or a different organization.

The arguments against the interpretive perspective rest largely on the difficulty of systematically representing the perceptions of others without falling into the trap of biasing the analysis with one's own subjective interpretation. This is quite apart from the inherent difficulties of the method itself, involving asking individuals to describe and account for their interpretive feelings. It is not self-evident that interpretive approaches necessarily avoid some of the criticisms which can be levelled at more structural analyses.

First, the interpretations of individuals are themselves located in a wider context. This broadening of context might be from individual organization to business sector; from business sector to overall national economic context, or from national context to questions of internationalization and differing national cultures (see Hofstede 1980, 1990; Tayeb 1989). The relative impact of context thus becomes an important dimension in shaping and being shaped by individuals' interpretation of any situation. Differences of position in hierarchy or in function in any one organization will as surely influence interpretations of events as differences in types of organization or nation states.

Second, the four interpretive steps laid out by Isabella (1990) are relatively close to the Lewin model of change (see chapters 2 and 3). There is still a strict temporal sequence implied, consisting largely of unfreezing, moving and refreezing the change process.

Finally, the emergence of patterns in individuals' interpretations can become confounded precisely because reality itself (as perceived) is an unfolding, changing factor. It is extremely difficult, therefore, to isolate and precisely identify those frames of reference which are conventional, or context-based, and those which are in the process of being formed (in-progress interpretation). The blurring of distinctions lends the interpretive perspective an air of inaccessibility. One can never know the absolute reality of others' interpretations and frames of reference.

Yet we should be careful not to dismiss the interpretive approaches as unattainable or as any less useful than structural approaches in analysing organizational change. Mangham's (1986) and Goffman's (1982) metaphor of drama allows us to see how individuals make sense of the dynamic of change through performance and drama. Isabella's (1990) analysis reminds us that the process of change is not just a sequence. It is a process fuelled by a variety of interpretations, each of which provides the spur to action, creates the vision and sustains the energies of those participants caught up in the process of change. Without cognition and interpretation the world of organizational change would be very bland indeed, a world of constantly identifying driving and restraining forces in order to alter the quasi-stationary equilibrium. Hardly the stuff of which organizational drama and transformation are made.

Interestingly, the counter-positioning of structural approaches to culture against the interpretive analysis just described leads to something of a dilemma. On the one hand, manipulating organizational culture in order to achieve some desired future state can be criticized roundly, since it makes simplistic assumptions about cause and effect and also requires individuals to change their behaviour in line with the demands of the 'new' culture. Yet interpretive analyses, which avoid the criticisms of simple causation, also founder on the rock of organizational context. It is this context which shapes individual perceptions, which allows the confirmation and shaping of ideas, and which ultimately leads to acceptance of or continued resistance to change. Thus it is too simplistic to divide cultural approaches into either structural or interpretive analyses. The two are at work simultaneously and both have to be considered as key factors in explaining both the processes and the outcomes of change.

Unfortunately for the student of change, this muddies the waters even further. For example, it is not just the interactions between individual behaviour, perception and organizational structure which need to be taken into account. The wider context in which the organization operates also casts its influence over both aspects (Greenwood and Hinings 1988).

THE WIDER ASPECTS OF CULTURE: SOCIETAL AND INSTITUTIONAL VALUES

So far we have examined conflicting analyses of the role of organizational culture in strategic change. However, we have also assumed so far that the appropriate unit of analysis is either the single individual or the single organization. As Di Maggio and Powell (1983) revealed, the external legitimization of change is an equally pervasive force in sustaining or destroying organizational transitions. Put simply, the extent to which changes conform to established patterns in the operating environment of the organization will determine greatly how change is hindered or facilitated and will also influence how changes are evaluated later on.

There appear to be at least two major factors to consider. The first concerns generalized norms in the environment. This could include norms of behaviour ranging from those within individual business sectors to those which characterize entire countries or geographical areas. The second concerns those patterns (structure, culture networks) which are set by market leaders in particular industries or service sectors.

Both factors have the concept of patterning central to their arguments. Taking patterning in business sectors first, Grinyer and Spender (1979) showed how organizations in particular niches or business sectors tend to adopt similar strategic responses when faced with pressure for change. They term this response managing by strategic 'recipes'. Such recipes become the yardstick by which the appropriateness of the response is judged by others in the sector. They also inevitably set limits around which alternatives for action are seriously considered and eventually implemented. Grinyer *et al.* (1987) studied twenty-six British companies over ten years. Those which had successfully managed to effect change (averting and turning round previous decline) were the organizations which had largely gone outside the recipes set by their respective industrial sectors. They had invested in training when others had thought it inappropriate. They had invested in people and technology, again running counter to previous practice in the sector. Table 3 gives some examples of these organizations.

Other aspects of patterning can be found in Greenwood and Hinings's (1988) idea of organizational design tracks. The argument is that organizations develop archetypes which embody where they

Table 5.1 British companies which achieved successful change by breaking away from strategic recipes

Arthur Bell & Sons	Macallan-Glenlivet
Associated Book Publishers	McCarthy & Stone
Associated Paper Industries	Pringle of Scotland
Collins Publishers	Rotaflex
Countryside Properties	Sidlaw Group
Dawson International	Sirdar
Don & Low	TI Group
Ellis & Goldstein Holdings	UDI Group
Ferranti	Ward White Group
Fisons	Whatman Reeve–Angel
Glaxo Holdings	John Wood Group
Low & Bonar	

Adapted from Grinyer *et al.* (1987)

are now and where they want to be in the future. The data which inform such archetypes come from various sources, although the actions of other organizations in the same business sector appear to be a major influence. Thus managers build up a set of beliefs, norms and cause–effect maps which represent a consistent pattern or design track for managing the organization in its wider environment. The change process is thus initiated. Along the way, different sets of patterns begin to emerge as managers modify their beliefs in the light of experience. These are then consolidated into a further archetype. As a theoretical piece of work Greenwood and Hinings's (1988) assertions require empirical evidence to lend support to the theory, although their categorization of tracks is intuitively appealing, as the following summary (adapted from Butler 1991: 242) shows:

1   *Inertia.* No change takes place. The organization remains true to its archetype, no matter what the stimuli towards change.

2   *Aborted excursions.* After an attempt to change, managers decide to give up and return to the *status quo.*

3   *Linear transformation.* Managers attempt to change; this involves some fragmentation in the organization (known as the schizoid phase) and eventually the change to another archetype is achieved.

4   *Oscillating transformation.* After a number of aborted excursions, or attempts at change, managers eventually decide upon another archetype. Many iterations may be involved in this process.

5   *Delayed transformation.* During the change process, interruptions and recycles occur, thus destroying much linearity. Nevertheless, a new archetype is persistently sought and is achieved in time.

6   *Unresolved excursions.* Begin like a linear transformation but get stuck, since managers are unable or cannot agree upon the characteristics of the new archetype.

One of the advantages of the above typology is that it provides a systematic comparative framework for empirical testing. It potentially allows change processes to be compared, something which has been noticeably absent from the general literature on organizational change, which either draws detailed data from a single case or lumps together seemingly endless examples of organizations which have changed their culture (Butler 1991). The only problem is that the measurement of culture often extends to hundreds of variables, obviating both comparisons and strongly significant results other than to say that culture is all things to all organizations.

Other examples of patterning are those of 'mimetic isomorphism' (Di Maggio and Powell 1983). Here the traditional organizational culture/excellence literature takes a further battering, since the argument focuses on the actions of market leaders, which are argued to influence organizational change, rather than the cultures of individual organizations or the desires and interests of individual managers. The basis of mimetic isomorphism is that of role modelling at the organizational level of analysis. Role modelling is more usually applied to the actions of individuals who model their behaviour upon other individuals whom they admire or respect. Individuals try to emulate the behaviour of those they admire in the hope of becoming like them and enjoying the rewards and benefits that are perceived to accrue. Such is also the case with organizations. According to Di Maggio and Powell (1983) organizational change can best be understood as a process of emulation in which market leaders or organizations with a 'good' reputation become the role models.

In an analysis of 292 organizations drawn from *Fortune*'s 1985 study of corporate reputations, Fombrun and Shanley (1990) show the potency of brand and market leaders in shaping subsequent changes for organizations operating in their business sectors. They cite (among others) Eastman Kodak, Merrill Lynch and Texas Instruments as organizations which have exerted an immense influence over others in their business sectors. Interestingly, potent reputations do not appear to be directly related to profitability. These three examples are indeed organizations which are well reputed and profitable. Less profitable but equally well reputed are PepsiCo, Polaroid and RCA. Their influence as role models is also strong.

The Fombrun and Shanley analysis gives some clues about organizational reputations. The authors argue that four factors seem to contribute to the external perception of a good reputation:

1 *Level of institutional ownership.* The greater the concentration of a firm's equity among institutions rather than individual share-holders the greater is its reputation.

2 *Social responsibility.* Essentially the non-economic face of organization; the better an organization responds (or is perceived to

respond) to social welfare or other corporate social responsibility issues the higher is its reputation.

3   *Level of media visibility.* The greater the direct media coverage
    (through radio, journalism, television) or the greater the indirect
    media visibility (through corporate ties such as interlocking
    directorates, etc.) the better is the organization's reputation.
    Media coverage can be either positive or negative – both kinds
    contribute to organizational reputation.

4   *Organizational size.* The larger the organization, generally, the
    better its reputation, possibly because it can manage public
    relations better than a smaller counterpart and, possibly,
    because larger organizations receive more media attention.

This sectoral perspective argues that individual organizational
culture is less important in understanding and achieving change
than the sector the company is in. Individual managers, too, are
likely to become locked into patterns of thinking which are substantially derived from the activities of leading organizations in the
relevant business sector.

A popular example of this was evident in the television
programme *Troubleshooter,* screened in Britain during 1989–90,
starring Sir John Harvey-Jones as change consultant to a wide range
of companies (including the NHS, Apricot Computers and Morgan
Cars). Even allowing for the editorial hand of the producer in
aiming to make 'good television', the consistency of Sir John's
approach was unmistakable, at least in my view. First look at the
balance sheet, identify strong and weak parts of the organization
from it, then sever the weak and nurture the strong and enhanced
performance will result. This recipe may or may not be effective.
Certainly, in the case of Apricot, deciding not to manufacture
computer assemblies any longer proved profitable, but persuading
an area health authority to be predominantly an economic profit-
driven business, or Morgan Cars to adopt mass-production/volume
output techniques, seemed a bizarre application of the recipe, somewhat blind to the wide differences in the values and ideologies of the
two organizations.

At an even more macro level of analysis, national characteristics
are equally important in the consideration of organizational change
through organizational culture. Despite the debates which relate to
whether or not national cultures have an impact upon organizational structures and processes, the likelihood is that the wide

array of factors which comprise any nation's culture will have some influence over how organizations and their managers think and act. Such factors include language, history, the political context, the legal context, religious beliefs and educational levels and practices, the values and attitudes of citizens and the preferred mode of social organization (e.g. hierarchical or co-operative and decentralized). Complete books and research projects have been dedicated to studying the impact of national cultures, so coverage of the topic is necessarily brief in this chapter. The work of Lammers and Hickson (1979), Hofstede (1980, 1990) and Tayeb (1989) represents the major debates, the first two authors arguing largely for convergence and the last two for divergence. The convergence thesis argues that organizations are becoming increasing alike, the business operating relatively independently of national context. The divergence thesis maintains that the differences in national context are substantial enough to influence the structures and processes of organizations in different countries.[2]

The relevance of these studies to organizational change is twofold. First, the patterning of national attitudes, values and beliefs closely parallels similar approaches to the culture of individual organizations. It's just that the levels of analysis are different. The same caveats should apply to each area of research, and care should be taken to avoid overgeneralized and stereotypical categorizations of cultures. Second, given the diversity of factors which contribute to shaping and fashioning national cultures, it is likely that one or more of these factors will act as a facilitator or as a hindrance to organizational change. This would obviously include such things as legal/fiscal factors, which might preclude joint ventures between companies in different countries (the aborted Midland Bank and Hong Kong & Shanghai Bank partnership is one example of this; the move was terminated after a three-year 'courtship'). Other less tangible factors would include a nation's history, its language or its political context.

Returning for a moment to the patterning of national cultures by clustering them along the lines of their similarity across a range of dimensions reveals some remarkable similarities between factors characterizing national cultural patterns and those factors used to describe organizational cultural patterns identified by Handy (1986). For example, Hofstede (1980, 1990) suggests four broad clusters of nations, based primarily on:

1   The prevailing sense of individualism or collectivity in each country.
2   The power distance accepted in each country (the degree of centralization, autocratic leadership, number of levels in hierarchy, etc.).
3   The degree to which uncertainty is tolerated or avoided.

The four broad clusters of countries are:

1   Scandinavia (primarily Denmark, Sweden and Norway). These cultures are based upon values of collectivity, consensus and decentralization.
2   West Germany (as it was pre-1990), Switzerland and Austria. These are grouped together largely as valuing efficiency – the well oiled machine – and seeking to reduce uncertainty.
3   Great Britain, Canada, the USA, New Zealand, Australia and the Netherlands. These are somewhere between (1) and (2) but cluster on the value they place on strong individuals and achievers in society.
4   Japan, France, Belgium, Spain and Italy. These are clustered on bureaucratic tendencies – a pyramid of people – favouring a large power distance.[3]

The similarity of factors in the national culture study to Handy's (1986) four organizational cultures is striking. Power cultures favour and nurture strong individuals; role cultures favour the pyramid of people as well as a large power distance and the reduction of ambiguity. Task cultures represent the decentralized, consensual organization which favours group working (collectivity) over individualism. Person cultures favour individualism, but avoid bureaucratization or large power distances.

The extent to which there are parallels between dominant national cultures and prevailing organizational cultures is a question for future research, although one could hypothesize that a consensus-based organizational culture which found itself in a 'bureaucratic' national culture would have a hard time remaining in that form (other things being equal). Thus we might look outside the·individual organization for pressures to change, or indeed outside the business sector of which it is part. Important clues might be found in the extent to which the dominant characteristics of national cultures pervade organizational structures and processes. Such an analysis would apply equally to multinational enterprises and to single-nation businesses.

SUMMARY

The simplistic notions of strong organizational cultures and associated organizational 'excellence' have been subjected to criticism in this chapter. The intellectual and methodological bases upon which such assumptions are founded are fundamentally flawed. This means that to effect change in an organization simply by attempting to change its culture assumes an unwarranted linear connection between something called organizational culture and performance. Not only is this concept of organizational culture multi-faceted, it is also not always clear precisely how culture and change are related, if at all, and, if so, in which directions.

Chapter 6

Programmed approaches to organizational change

Until this point there has been relatively little mention of programmed approaches to organizational change. The term 'programmed' (fashionable in North America and gaining popularity in Britain) is used here to denote those approaches which concentrate upon the 'how' of change rather than the 'what' (processual or outcome-oriented). To some extent the purely applied aspects of organizational culture (see chapter 5) can be viewed as a programme of change, although there are a number of other programmes which are designed more explicitly to be the tools of organizational change. In this chapter we discuss some of the major programmed approaches to organizational change. The discussion covers a number of levels of analysis. First, programmes aimed at individual organizations are examined, specifically looking at total quality management packages. Second, programmes for individual managers are outlined, including management training and development packages. Then the analysis focuses on the more macro concerns of strategic co-operation and finally discusses the economics of deregulation and privatization as programmes for change. First, we examine the question of Total Quality Management.

PROGRAMMES AIMED AT INDIVIDUAL ORGANIZATIONS

Total Quality Management

If there is anything to rival the extent to which organizational culture has permeated questions of organizational transformation, it is perhaps the concept of Total Quality Management (TQM). It is difficult to encounter any medium or large organization in Britain, North America or continental Europe which has not already

installed some variation of TQM as the cornerstone of its transformation. Total Quality Management, like all programmes of
change, makes it possible to talk plausibly about a strategy of
change. Change is oriented towards a specific goal which can be
articulated and which can be achieved via a planned programme of
steps. Yet precisely what is TQM? And is it going to deliver the
seemingly transformed organization capable of superior competitive
performance in the 1990s and beyond?

First, it is important to recognize that TQM is not just a
programme for quality in the 'traditional' sense meant by manufacturing quality control and the reduction of scrap or wastage in
inventory processing. TQM is a concept applicable to the whole
organization. It is a philosophy and a set of techniques aimed at
creating and maintaining a constancy of purpose towards the
improvement of products and services. The basis of TQM is cross-
functional co-operation, largely through sales and marketing inter-
acting with production, coupled with an obsession about quality
service for the customer. There are a range of total quality packages
available. Some of the main approaches are summarized below:

Major systems from the USA:

1   *Phil Crosby*: fourteen steps based upon the philosophy of 'zero
    defects'.
2   *Joe Juran*: Very similar to Crosby, based upon the 'right first
    time' principle.
3   *Richard Deming*: fourteen steps, based upon the removal of
    organizational quotas and controls and replacing them with
    leaders, and increased training for managers.
4   *The Conway system*: six steps, based upon 'imagineering', i.e.
    looking into the future and asking, 'What if?'

Major systems from the UK:

5   *PA Consultants* : very similar to Crosby and Deming.
6   *David Hutchins Associates*: based upon the extensive use of
    quality circles.

Whilst there are differences in method between the TQM packages, their overall philosophies are very similar. Deming's (1986)
fourteen points for management are highly representative of the
programmed step-by-step approach to organizational transformation which characterizes these approaches. Deming calls the transformation process a 'virtuous circle' in which defining customer

needs becomes paramount, the task of management being to translate those needs into operational terms for all parts of the organization (see fig. 7). Specific improvements in quality emerge not from the individual elements of fig. 7 (e.g increased market share, or cost reduction) but from transformations in the processes which link all the elements together. It is worth summarizing Deming's philosophy in achieving this link to show the extent to which such approaches permeate the whole organization, its strategy, philosophy and its management.

The stepwise approach to TQM is common to many programmes and is central to Deming's approach. The philosophical basis of TQM is rooted in the contention that business organizations in the west have been characterized by knee-jerk short-termism in their strategic response to change in the face of environmental demands. Instead of looking to the long term, managers have been encouraged to become preoccupied with short-term pressures. One of the outcomes of this process has arguably been the emergence of competitive behaviour within and between organizations at the expense of teamwork and co-operation. One of the guiding principles in achieving TQM is redressing the balance between teamwork and co-operation and competition. This may involve individuals forgoing short-term gains in the pursuit of corporate goals. All functions, particularly marketing research, design, sales and production, should be brought together under the banner of co-operation.

Figure 6.1 Towards transformation via the virtuous circle of quality (adapted from Deming 1986)

In order to achieve this, some fundamental reorganizations of organizational processes and individual ways of doing things are required to change. For example, business should neither be sought nor awarded solely on the basis of price. Instead, organizations should look to reduce and minimize total costs. An ultimate aim is to move towards using a single supplier for specific items based upon a long-term relationship of trust and loyalty. The reduction of internally generated costs can be monitored via statistical process control (SPC) and from customer feedback (market research, the cost of warranty claims, etc.). Empirical support for this step derives from Scherkenbach (1988), who argues that, if price becomes the final arbiter, low quality and high prices become inevitable. Long-term contracts with suppliers allow them to plan strategically for the future without having to worry about losing business (by being undercut on price, for example). Similarly, the supplier is, in theory, motivated towards constant improvement in meeting the needs of the client over the years.

Interestingly, this is no new concept. In 1926, when the first Volvo car was assembled in Sweden, the organization was based upon informal long-term relationships with suppliers, as well as with other subcontractors, upon whom Volvo was to remain highly dependent for almost thirty-five years (Kinch 1988). Not all suppliers were to remain in a position to retain their strategies, however. The engine supplier was acquired in 1930, as was the firm which produced truck gearboxes in 1941. Only the supplier of sheet steel for body panels was to remain independent for over thirty years, with a supply contract based upon a handshake and trust (Kinch 1988). So it would seem at least from this example that suppliers might think twice about entering into long-term contracts if the likely result is to be taken over or merged with their client company. This is likely to be especially the case if the client company experiences massive growth and economic success (as in the Volvo case). There are also data from research on inter-organizational dependences which present a convincing case against creating a situation where one organization deliberately becomes dependent upon another, with no easy substitute to hand (Hickson *et al.* 1971; Hinings *et al.* 1974). The point is developed later in this chapter.

The more processual aspects of TQM appear in the later steps of the Deming programme. Here the task is to examine the organization and to test it against the criteria laid down in the previous steps. Is the organization aiming for the long term? Is the question of quality uppermost in the minds of managers? Are suppliers seen more as trusted friends than as antagonistic organizations in the political arena of business? This done, the process should recycle until the greatest level of fit is obtained between what is and what should be according to the theory. Factors which may help the organization achieve the transformation to TQM include:

1   The elimination of quotas for shop-floor employees.
2   The elimination of Management by Objectives (MBO).
3   The removal of any obstacles which come between the worker and pride of workmanship. This means changed roles for both supervisors and workers so that all workers can feel driven not by annual merit ratings and production quotas but by having achieved, in their own terms, a high standard of workmanship.
4   Instilling in all individuals that quality is their responsibility. The mission of TQM and the transformation of the organization are everyone's job.

Whilst we might agree in principle with the above statements as organizational 'desiderata' it is by no means clear how this state of TQM is to be achieved – at least from reading the literature on the subject (see Oakland 1989). Yet the very solutions put forward by advocates of TQM cover familiar and contentious terrain for the student of organizational change. We examine these in turn in the subsequent sections of this chapter.

The central role of leadership

Of course, it is not just in the TQM philosophies that we can find the argument that the drastic reduction of organizational controls and the installation of teamwork places greater emphasis upon leaders and leadership (Bryman 1986; Hosking 1988). However, the *extent* to which TQM advocates effective leadership as a substitute for organizational structure, hierarchy and controls is remarkable. The arguments against organizational controls are familiar enough from traditional industrial sociology. Quotas, for example, are argued to be barriers to continuous improvement, since once a worker attains the quota he or she is rarely motivated to try further. (Much empirical data from motivation theories would also support this view.) Management by Objectives equally produces often spurious sets of objectives which encourage managers to play the numbers game (i.e. targets are set and met in much the same way that financial systems encourage managers to work to budgets and little else, see chapter 4).

The remedy, according to TQM, is effective leadership. There are individuals who know how objectives can and should be met. They emphasize quality rather than numbers and empower people to perform to the best of their ability. Leaders are allowed to play the 'fear game' only so long as they base their arguments on organizational survival (e.g. 'We will soon go out of business if we cannot reduce costs by x per cent'). Finally, managers (as leaders, so this also includes supervisors and team leaders) should seek the causes of poor performance from factors other than human variability in an otherwise 'fixed' system of technology and products. Part of this leadership style is, therefore, to drive out fear from individuals and create an atmosphere of mutual trust. Deming (1986) cites examples of the dysfunctions of fear, most of which appear to have been caused by leaders insisting that failures were predominantly human in origin and that poor performance could be rectified by resort to hierarchical power to tell subordinates what to do. Poor performance includes 'whitewashing activities' where, because of a lack of security in the job, individuals cover their tracks or engage in intense and visible activity in an attempt to satisfy the demands of more senior management. Resistance to new knowledge and technology also represents poor performance, since any response to change will inevitably be sluggish. Finally, dysfunctions can occur in the informal organization via robust and active grape vines coupled with the tendency for information to be filtered in any communication.

Again, there appears to be nothing new in these elements that traditional industrial sociology could not have taught us. Yet the insistence that effective leadership is a key route to achieving changes on these dimensions is relatively novel. Such faith, however, would seem a little off-target, given the paucity of knowledge, the intense level of conceptual disagreement and the apparent gaps in knowledge in the general field of leadership theories. From this perspective, it appears to be a case of blind faith. In response, most of the TQM advocates argue that managers can be trained to be leaders (we deal with this issue in the next section), although this, too, raises more questions than it seems to answer.

The primary problem with substituting effective leaders for quotas and other organizational controls seems to be that no one can agree precisely what is meant by the term 'leadership'. To some it is a characteristic of the individual – at the extreme a trait which some possess and others do not. To others, leadership is more a function of picking appropriate styles to suit varying contingent circumstances in the organization or the group (see House 1971, Vroom and Yetton 1973, for example). There are those who argue that leadership *per se* does not exist independently of social action, arguing that leadership is predominantly a social process characterized by networking and social skill (Hosking 1990). Finally there are those who argue the leadership is largely a redundant concept which could be replaced in most organizations by aspects of individuals, the tasks carried out and the organization itself (see the discussion by Thompson and McHugh 1990: 345–9). The ability, experience, training, motivation and independence of individuals will to a great extent determine whether they 'need' leadership or would react favourably to being led (Lynne 1966). So, too, will the extent to which the task is innately satisfying, is subject to variety, is tied down to the specific technology in use and is relatively autonomous (see Scarbrough and Corbett 1992 in this series). Finally, the structure, culture, selection processes and reward systems of any organization can effectively reduce the need for leadership, especially the 'John Wayne in pinstripes' model favoured by some of the more evangelical change theorists (Thompson and McHugh 1990: 229). Thus the relative need for leaders is likely to vary at least by organizational type, by technology-in-use and by the kind of tasks performed. Two striking examples come from the empirical study of the British voluntary sector by Butler and Wilson (1990: 116–30, 108–16). The first, that of the Royal National Institute for the Blind (RNIB), shows the difficulties that can arise from deliberately bringing in leaders to turn an organization round. The second, that of Christian Aid (CAID), illustrates that changes in organizational structure can eliminate the need for leadership throughout a large part of the organization.

Founded in 1868, the RNIB grew into a large, bureaucratic organization with some twenty-five different functions ranging from Braille publications to sound-recording, vocational services and public appeals departments. In an attempt to make the organization more effective in service delivery and in managerial performance (TQM) a new Director General (Ian Bruce) was appointed from outside the voluntary sector in November 1983. Within a year the need for leadership had been identified, and new directors were appointed to take charge of the now pared-down five functions.

Including the post of Director General, 50 per cent of the appointments were new and came from commercial organizations or from the public sector. All seemed set for a trouble-free organizational change, but the heavy hand of history and of organizational ideology was to frustrate the new directors in achieving their goals of efficiency and effective performance. There was no ready access to data (on either givers or receivers of services). Financial data were patchy. Decisions still took a long time to process, going through a series of committees (a hangover from the past). The market was changing at the same time (the major client body is ageing and likely to have multiple handicaps in addition to visual problems). Yet, whilst the new directors had the strategic autonomy to effect change, they were confounded by an organization which seemed tenaciously to cling to the old ways of doing things, effectively frustrating attempts at change through new leadership.

Christian Aid is a relatively new British charity, being around fifty years old, a child of the British Council of Churches. Its aims are to combat disease, malnutrition, distress and sickness throughout the world under the broad banner of a Christian philosophy. Like many charities operating in Third World overseas aid, CAID grew rapidly into a large organization (over 200 staff) with a bureaucratic structure. In April 1986 the organization attempted structural change on a grand scale. The change was from a bureaucratic to a decentralized matrix structure. This was coupled with a change of Director, who was brought in to manage the new matrix structure. In theory the change should have brought flexibility, proactivity and efficiency. In practice great difficulties were experienced for over two years whilst individuals became used to the new structure and its different demands. Primarily, those who had previously been leaders of departments lower down the organization now had their role changed. There was not such a need for so many leaders. This was coupled with an increasingly formalized role description for all employees, effectively reducing the autonomy many had enjoyed in their jobs. Whilst the structure conformed to TQM principles, the ways in which individuals perceived what the change meant for them (especially the erosion of autonomy and reduction in departmental leadership) created a host of problems from which the organization is only now beginning to emerge.

It seems that blanket programmed change strategies such as TQM need to be able to adapt to the highly differentiated needs posed by different types of organization if they are to be anything other than a very general vocabulary of vague organizational improvements.

The focus on leadership also raises political questions in the processes of organizational change. Specifically, this means that relying on leaders to be fully in harmony with the new TQM scenario would appear to be unrealistic. Leaders exercise power in organizations. To the extent that they deviate from the prescriptive norms laid down by the TQM programme that power can be used to detract from the original purpose of the programme.

For example, the roles into which leaders are placed are likely to affect the ways in which they welcome or resist changes through TQM. In multi-national corporations such as Nestlé, leadership style is very much decentralized throughout the Strategic Business Units around the world. But ultimate power to sanction changes in SBU policies lies with headquarters in Switzerland, effectively constraining the actions of SBU leaders. This means that suggestions from SBU leaders are often rejected, or action is delayed, until headquarters makes up its mind. In organizations such as British Petroleum or British Telecom which are striving towards increased customer service (one of Deming's steps), the power of senior management to slow down or block the transition is potent. These organizations are the product of many years' business experience; as a result they are largely product-oriented, and have senior managers who perhaps grew up with this kind of business. Achieving change in these kinds of organizations requires more than just the application of a programmed package such as TQM. Something else has to make it work. As one manager from the National Westminster Bank observed during a training course on TQM, 'Most of the staff at middle and junior management levels are motivated to get involved and give it (TQM) a try, but senior managers endlessly ask these staff to do a whole host of other things not related to TQM.' Often such tasks occur in organizations which are facing major changes, where short-term solutions or fire-fighting management become the rule and aiming for survival (rather than quality) becomes the norm.

A further factor which can confound the efficacy of packages goes back to the question of organizations and their history. For example, in organizations where previously decentralization into SBUs has been attempted with less than successful results, the chances of achieving this through wrapping-up decentralization in the vocabulary of total quality is unlikely to work. Many organizations in the

British financial services sector would fit this description, short-term financial pressures resulting in decentralization being either short-lived or operating in name only as control is sought from centralized senior management.

Drawing upon interviews (conducted between 1987 and 1990) with a sample of eighty managers drawn from nine organizations (STC–ICL, Cadbury–Schweppes, National Westminster Bank, Midland Bank, Nestlé, Eagle Star, GEC–Plessey Telecommunications, the Co-operative Union and British Steel) enabled the following criticisms of change programmes through TQM to be compiled. Each organization had a change programme in place. The interviews asked respondents how they felt the programme helped or hindered the strategic change efforts which were being made in each organization. The sample of managers was chosen from those who had attended executive and senior management courses at the University of Warwick between 1987 and 1990. All respondents were directly involved in change programmes in their own organization. The following represents an analysis of the responses, gathered together under the major themes (i.e. those issues which received most mention from respondents). They are listed in descending order of number of mentions across the sample.

1 *Intangible benefits.* TQM is good at creating plenty of activity, but it is difficult to measure its benefits other than ultimately getting British Standard 5750 (ISO 9000). In many respects, the change programme becomes one of jumping through hoops in order to achieve the standard, which may be useful as a competitive advantage over organizations which offer the same product or service but which are unable to advertise the British Standard of quality. The amount of organizational change which occurs can become largely irrelevant in this pursuit.

2 *Sectional interests.* TQM can create 'evangelists' among those managers who are its (often) fanatical supporters. This can lead to fragmentation in any organization between those who support the programme and those who view it with less enthusiasm. In time this can create the kind of 'local rationality' which Cyert and March (1963) argued to be so detrimental to effective decision-making in organizations.

3 *The customer comes first and is also the judge.* Whilst staying close to the customer and developing a customer-oriented perspective may be laudable goals in their own right, ultimately whether or

not TQM programmes are judged a success or not lies directly with the customer and is effectively out of the hands of those internal managers who seek to control it. This can serve to demotivate those who perhaps were its original supporters when the programme was first introduced.

4   *The sponge phenomenon.* Large-scale change programmes like TQM can easily become all-embracing processes into which virtually all organizational problems are put. In some cases, the programme has little hope of solving the problems and so is judged to have failed despite not being designed to handle everything in the first place. The programme can soak up more problems than it can realistically handle.

5   *Recreating the rigid organization.* Because the programme requires absolute commitment throughout the organization, in the cases where it is achieved TQM is deemed to have been a success. Yet this is when it is at its most dangerous as far as future changes are concerned. The outcomes of a successful TQM programme can create a very comfortable *status quo* from which further change proves very difficult.

6   *The distinction between means and ends becomes blurred.* The programme can easily slip into becoming an end in itself rather than a means to an end (i.e. creating an organizational change for better economic performance). This is particularly true of programmes which require sequential steps to be fulfilled before embarking on the next set of changes. Achieving the steps becomes the end in itself rather than the means to systematic organizational change.

7   *TQM can make things worse.* Paradoxically, change programmes like TQM require that the organization is in a reasonable state of health to begin with. By this, respondents usually mean that there is enough organizational 'slack' (see chapter 5) to allow space for the programme to work. For those organizations which most needed massive strategic changes (i.e. those which are close to crisis), applying programmes could help seal the demise of the already declining organization. This is more true of organizations which are in a state of absolute rather than relative decline (see McKiernan 1992 in this series).

8   *Lack of evidence.* Finally, there appears to be a general lack of empirical evidence of change programmes deemed to have been successful (in Britain and Europe at least). There appear to be two reasons: (a) the programmes are heavily derived from

manufacturing organizations and experience and do not always translate directly into service organizations of various kinds; (b) the change programme is rigid in terms of ability to adapt to differences in international operations – it proved not to take into account any differences in national cultures (see chapter 5).

PROGRAMMES FOR INDIVIDUAL MANAGERS

A programme for change through management training

Common to both TQM and to installing leaders as agents of change lie the programmes and philosophies of management training and development. The basic idea underlying the emphasis on management training is that managers who have undergone a programme of training are in a strong position to act as agents of change as well as being able to understand more fully the complexities of organizational change from an analytical perspective. In this section, training and development are discussed together, although analytically it should be borne in mind that they are different. Training refers to a systematic set of processes, often supplied by training organizations, in which an individual learns specific skills and knowledge. In turn, these develop knowledge so that he or she can better achieve both personal and organizational goals. Development places the onus of learning squarely on the individual. Training organizations may help guide the process, but ultimately learning is derived from the individual asking questions, confronting new situations and coming to his or her own conclusions. We treat these two extreme approaches together here (there are a whole host of stages between training and development), since the primary aim of both is to produce managers who can understand and effect organizational change.

One of the ironies in writing about management training in a book like this is that the challenges posed to individuals by rapid and diverse organizational changes have led to a massive demand for training courses which help individuals to cope with and manage change processes. In many ways, one could argue that, since the challenge of change is one of the key *raisons d'être* of the book, it should have begun with questions of training. The reason it does not is simple. As we shall see, training (especially that part of it dedicated to managers) is characterized by a predominantly 'how to' approach. Training can thus be considered a programme. For example, change produces symptoms of stress in some individuals, so training involves a programme of 'how to cope' strategies which range from physiological recipes (check your diet, take more exercise) to psychological approaches (meditate, develop a new 'mind set' which places change in perspective) and so on. Specifically for managers, training for change involves a similar set of recipes – how to cope with; how to keep up with; how to manage and how to manage others in the processes of change. Yet none of these questions the fundamental nature of change itself. To learn, we first have to understand what it is we are training for. Indeed, that is one of the central lessons of many training courses on change – first define the goal – but the message seems to have been lost in the current rush towards educating managers to handle organizational change.

The emergence of the current programmes of management training in Britain has been well documented elsewhere (Sadler 1989; Constable and McCormick 1987; Handy 1987; Mangham and Silver 1986). Beginning slowly after the Second World War, management education as we know it today, with close links between industry and business schools, has really only developed significantly since the 1960s. The history of the emergence of the UK business schools makes fascinating reading (Sadler 1989) but, for the purposes of this book, we shall concentrate on the state of management education today as it especially relates to questions of organizational change.

It is, of course, no accident that the content of management training programmes closely reflects the paradigms prevailing in management theory at the time. Training, too, has to be considered in context. All Taylor's managers needed to be trained in was a set of goal-directed principles. Since everything was rational, all managers needed to do was to clarify the goal (almost always this was 100 per cent efficiency from workers who were to be totally dedicated to greater production volumes). For those workers who only worked at 75 per cent efficiency, the management task was to replace them with others who could produce better figures. No talk here of dismissal procedures and counselling for employees, nor of motivation and job satisfaction, which were to emerge as the content of management training when the era of the human relations school dawned (some twenty-five years later). It is all too easy to talk of Taylorism as if it were long past. Yet many organizations view current management training (which talks of employee involvement, caring and sharing environments and the value of the human resource) as icing on the otherwise substantial cake of Tayloristic principles. 'Getting the goods out of the door fast and furious is all that matters,' as one manufacturing manager observed to me during his training course. The date was 1991. Another example of the persistence of Taylorism from my own experience in the 1960s will live with me for ever.

There were not many options open to unemployed individuals or to those 'between jobs' (like myself) to earn substantial amounts of money in a relatively short time. One was provided by a firm which specialized in the freezing and packing of all kinds of meat and vegetables. The real money came by working in the 'pea season', a period of six weeks in which peas were picked, delivered to the cold store, boiled lightly (blanched), checked for quality, graded by thickness of skin and size, fast-frozen in huge refrigerated hoppers and then bagged in 56 lb sacks, to be stored in large freezer rooms for the big frozen food companies. Shifts were twelve hours per day, seven days per week. The organization employed a variety of labour: some were students, others were recently released prisoners from the nearby gaol (which mainly housed violent offenders).

My job was to stand at the bottom of one of the refrigeration hoppers with an open bag. I would shout 'Peas,' and someone would open the chute. When I judged the bag was full, I would shout 'Stop!' and pass the bag on for weighing and loading on to pallets. This went on around the clock for six weeks. The managers' jobs were entirely those of policemen and supervisors. They stood behind workers and directly measured their efficiency by counting the number of bags, or the volume of peas, etc. Those not performing to target were hauled off the line and instantly dismissed. In some cases this resulted in quite a degree of physical violence against the 'pillocks' (as the supervisory staff were affectionately known). Managers not only had to know how to count bags, but had to be effective pugilists as well. Finally, workers hardly dared leave their position for fear of dismissal through shirking, even to go to the toilet. I have never knowingly eaten a frozen pea since I discovered that workers on the blanchers (large open boilers) would sometimes urinate into the boiler rather than risk dismissal by going to the toilets.

Whilst the above example shows the persistence of Taylorism, it also shows what management skills were valued in the factory. You had to be hard, tough and able to count. Management training for these kind of jobs was virtually non-existent, nor was it actively sought.

The advent of the informal organization and the demise of some of Taylorism did bring with it the need to add to the managerial skill repertoire. The idea of productivity through people was born and a host of managerial techniques for motivating, leading and coaching were on the training menu. Yet, in Britain, very few managers were to enter the realms of management training at all. According to Keep (1989) British managers in 1987 received an average of one day's formal training and the majority of managers received no training at all.

The consequence appears to have been an unprecedented effort for management training to figure as an important aspect of a manager's job. As in the USA, in the UK these efforts have resulted in a remarkably homogeneous approach towards management training, a large portion of which focuses precisely on the management of change. Homogeneity is achieved by what has become known generally as the competence frameworks. Managers are argued to need certain competences (e.g. being able to work in a team) the sum total of which leads to effective management generally and the ability to handle and manage change specifically. As an example of competences from the USA, Quinn *et al.* (1990) produced a list of competences mastery of which, they argue, will produce the 'master' manager:

1   The *director* role. Taking the initiative. Goal setting. Effective delegation.
2   The *producer* role. Personal productivity and motivation. Time and stress management. Motivating others.
3   The *co-ordinator* role. Planning, organizing, controlling.
4   The *monitor* role. Writing effectively. Reducing information overload.
5   The *mentor* role. Understanding oneself and others. Effective interpersonal communication. Developing subordinates.
6   The *facilitator* role. Team building. Participative decision-making. Conflict management.
7   The *innovator* role. Creative thinking. Living with and managing change.
8   The *broker* role. Creating and maintaining a power base. Effective negotiation and influencing skills. Effective oral presentation.

By splitting management tasks up into eight competences Quinn *et al.* (1990) present a confusing picture of what are the key areas for management training. Their division of the management task into eight roles is based upon the notion of 'competing values' in which, for example, a manager of the Taylorist school would need the competences which fall under the 'director' and 'producer' roles. Managers with a penchant for the human relations style need the competences which fall under the 'co-ordinator' and 'mentor' roles, and so on.

The argument broadly is that all-round competence to handle the dynamics of change comes from a programme of training in which individuals learn each of the competences. Interestingly, Quinn *et al.* are very unforthcoming when they come to discuss the competence which deals explicitly with managing change (the role of the 'innovator' – see the list above. The authors tell us that 'this is one of the most compelling, and yet least understood, of the eight leadership roles' (Quinn *et al.* 1990: 237). They go on to deal in a rather prescriptive way, with linking organizational culture, creative thinking and the ability to add and subtract forces for and against change from a Lewinian model of change. The quote, too, is telling. It makes an explicit link between management training via the attainment of competences and leadership. According to this point of view, good leaders are those who possess most of the competences. As we have seen earlier in this chapter, leadership is not solely about the possession of competences. It is a process of social exchange between leader and follower, located in a complex web of organizational and societal contexts. Just being 'competent' is not enough.

Furthermore, Quinn *et al.* (1990: 316), under the rather odd title which omits the word 'manager' and consequently reads 'the profile of the master' (could this be popular science fiction?), state that, for a manager to become trained in order to handle change, 'first is the ability to play all eight roles at least at a competent level. Second is the ability to blend and balance the competing roles in an appropriate way' (*sic*). They cite empirical evidence (mostly from a working paper of Quinn and others) of 'balanced' and 'unbalanced' profiles of competences, which are relatively more or less effective for handling change (and developing leadership). Now, from what we have covered so far in our analysis of change, we must cast serious doubt on the competence form of training. No mention is made of the degree of change, of the different contexts and antecedents which surround the process. Is change viewed as a process at all, or is it a goal or an outcome? When does a manager know how to 'switch on' his or her 'appropriate' competences? It would require an enormous degree of situational analysis before even a tentative decision could be made about appropriateness. Time lags, coupled with supposed cause-and-effect relationships in the mind of the individual, will also have an influence over the choice of appropriate roles or competences. The world of the master manager presented by Quinn *et al.*, however, seems free from uncertainty, is eminently predictable, and suffers from none of those annoying political issues which other managers find confound even their best intentions (see Lukes 1974; Hickson *et al.* 1986).

Before examining Quinn *et al.*'s approach further, what of the UK? Can we find better examples of training programmes designed to help managers facilitate change? The answer is that, in recent years, there has been a tremendous effort both by government and by training institutions (in the private and public educational sectors) to provide such programmes. Unfortunately, the programmes at the centre of this activity come pretty close to resembling the Quinn *et al.* approach. Indeed, there seems no escape from the notion of competences, since they are the basis of the Management Charter Initiative (MCI) arguably the most complete and powerful programme of training to emerge in the field of UK management.

The management charter initiative

The basic philosophy of this training package (introduced in 1987–8 but not yet fully implemented) is that competitive advantage is gained by keeping organizations dynamic, flexible and open to change. Neither technology nor sophisticated management information systems are given much credence by the MCI in achieving this. Instead, the argument is that it is managers who facilitate flexibility and change. The key skills to learn are those of interpersonal relations, motivation, leadership and 'people skills' in general. A new body, the Council for Management Education and Development, was set up as an umbrella body to co-ordinate the MCI, although there are a number of disputes as to which body ought to run the programme. The structure of the bodies which contribute towards the programme is shown in fig. 8.

The aims of the programme are to systematize management

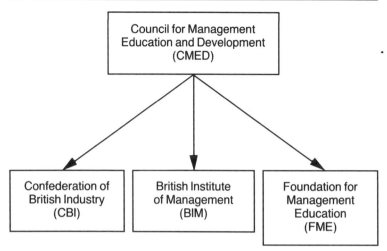

Figure 6.2 The bodies that run the Management Charter Initiative. Following the Constable and McCormick report (1987), this structure was set up. Its aims were to: **1** promote the mass support of higher management standards in UK companies (the initiative), **2** develop a recognized system of management qualifications (the charter), **3** form a Chartered Institute of Management to run the initiative (professionalization)

education in Britain. Since many managers appeared to have no formal training at all, instead learning by the 'school of hard knocks' (Keep 1989), the MCI was at first warmly welcomed. The initiative aims to promote across-the-board support for higher standards of management education in British organizations. The charter was to develop a recognized system of specifically management qualifications which were to be drawn up under the aegis of a Chartered Institute of Management. The ultimate broad aim is the professionalization of managers so that they can cope with, direct, and draw benefit from the turbulence of organizational change. The past tense is used occasionally above because the MCI ran into difficulties and the implementation of the programme has been somewhat delayed. (Whether the delay is terminal for the Initiative remains to be seen.)

From a high point of optimism at the outset, when approximately 350 organizations supported the charter (led vociferously by Bob Reid, then chairman of Shell and now of British Rail) endless problems have arisen about the MCI as a programme of change itself. For example, the notion of a universal list of competences appeared alien to a number of managers and to their companies.

Many companies which supported the charter initially began to press for the competences to be 'tailored' to suit the demands of their particular business. (These organizations included those in the financial services sector, telecommunications and brewing, among others.) The tendency to assume that every business is unique, and to exert pressure for course syllabuses to be tailored, will be no surprise to any reader who runs an educational programme (e.g. MBAs) supported by one or more organizations. Understandably, each organization wants its specific problems addressed in the syllabus.

Empirical evidence does not support the uniqueness argument at all. In the private sector, Grinyer *et al.* (1987) showed that corporate successes after strategic turn-around had manifestly common themes across a wide range of businesses. Their sample covered twenty-six firms in the public and private sectors. Hickson *et al.* (1986) also demonstrated that there were no significant differences between public and private organizations in the characteristics of their strategic decision-making processes, again running counter to a number of strong stereotypical images. The sample covered 150 cases of strategic decision-making in thirty organizations (with an equal split between public and private ownership). Finally, in the voluntary sector, Butler and Wilson (1990) examined the strategy and structure of thirty-one UK charities and concluded that there were more problems in common with organizations in other sectors than differences. Yet the notion often held by very senior managers that their organization is unique and faces unique problems is curiously pervasive. Assumptions of uniqueness by managers and the philosophy of a broad programme of change through management education run directly counter to one another. In the final analysis, they are probably mutually exclusive.

Further problems with MCI as a programme of change emerge when time frames are considered. The aims of the MCI are long-term. Yet the dominant strategies of organizations tend to be short-term. (Hickson *et al.* 1986 showed that it was rare for senior managers to think beyond twelve months in strategic decision-making, and John Banham, currently heading the CBI, has been heard many times to lament the apparently British industrial disease of short-termism.

Intellectually it is extremely disappointing that both the MCI and the competences approach of Quinn *et al.* (1990) have hardly moved away from the programme of management development proposed by Blake and Mouton in 1964. Figure 9 depicts their 'managerial grid'. The grid lists those aspects of management which are mostly concerned with production and those which are mostly concerned with people. In theory, eighty-one different combinations of styles are possible, but the five main contrasting styles are depicted in fig. 9. Essentially, Blake and Mouton's argument is that the manager

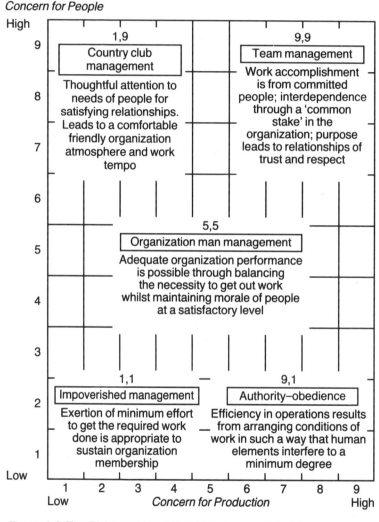

Figure 6.3 The Blake and Mouton (1964) managerial grid

who is well developed (i.e. can cope with change and is capable of taking his or her organization into the realms of superior performance) is the 9,9 team manager, who is equally concerned with getting the goods out of the door as with the people who manufacture them.

The trouble is, according to Blake and Mouton, that the majority of managers can be found along the diagonal of the grid running from country club management, through organization man/woman to authority–obedience. It is not that managers are actively coping with organizational change in a planned or systematic way. Rather, change forces differences in management style to suit circumstances. For example, when times are good and the market is stable (or competition is weak) many managers adopt a country club style. As soon as the market tightens up, competition increases and the general operating environment becomes more hostile, then managers tend to adopt the authority–obedience style. By way of compromise, the majority tend to fall into the middle category (5,5), conforming with organizational cultures and rules, playing it safe and never putting their head above the parapet in case it is shot off.

In sum, the competences programmes of the 1980s and 1990s have done or said little new beyond what we could have known or gleaned from the managerial grid. The grid contains the rational-production competences and also embraces the human-centred competences. Of course, the grid never specifies precisely what each individual competence comprises but it is disappointing to reflect that the production of such a (still contentious) list may have been the principal outcome of around twenty years of programmatic change through management training.

MACRO-STRUCTURAL PROGRAMMES OF CHANGE: JOINT VENTURES AND STRATEGIC ALLIANCES – STRATEGIES OF CO-OPERATION

In marked contrast to the programmes of individual development and change, macro-structural programmes take a broad organizational view. Change in these cases is facilitated by organizations working together towards some common aim rather than by competing on an individual basis. Such a programme of change is relatively new. There is, as yet, sparse empirical evidence to demonstrate the greater efficacy of strategic co-operation over strategic competition, yet we can draw some tentative conclusions, both from work which outlines the disadvantages of strategic competition and hints at the advantages of co-operation, and from the sparse empirical literature on co-operative strategies.[1]

A wealth of empirical data indicates that organizational success is not just a function of adopting a particular strategic profile of competition. The organizational changes so induced must have a congruent, supporting framework of organizational structures and processes which facilitate the chosen strategy (see Miller and Friesen 1984; Pettigrew *et al.* 1989). In a comparison of successful and unsuccessful commercial firms, Miller and Friesen (1984), Snow and Hrebiniak (1983) and Bartlett *et al.* (1990) found that:

1   Piecemeal attempts at following a competitive strategy invariably fail. Particular decision topics cannot be singled out as those which are innovative and competitive whilst the rest of the organization goes about its day-to-day business. The entire organization must be behind the competitive strategy in all respects.

2   Following point 1, competitive strategies appear ultimately to require the support of centralized, formal and functional structures, even if they begin life as decentralized, team-based organizations. The demands of economies of scale and of increasing complexity put immense pressure upon organizations to centralize the co-ordination and control of their competitive strategies.

3   Competitive strategies, by definition, preclude the possibility of co-operation or alliances between organizations as an alternative.

Many managers have already recognized the strategic choice of co-operation and are beginning to reorganize around co-operative strategies (termed, variously, joint ventures or strategic alliances). The myth that all commercial organizations are competing with cut-throat intensity persists, nevertheless (see Byars 1984). In a survey of strategic alliances between previously competing companies in North America, Lewis (1990) identified approximately a hundred cases of joint ventures. Japanese industry has worked on the maxim of co-operation with suppliers, customers and peer organizations for many years (Goldenberg 1988).

The pursuit of competitive strategies leads naturally towards contracting relationships and competitive bidding between organizations. This might be relatively easy and 'natural' for private, commercial organizations but is much more of a problem for both statutory and voluntary organizations. Competitive strategies, therefore, may be attractive initially to managers from one section of the economy but not to managers from other parts of the economy. Concern over this from, for example, the National Health Service and from the voluntary sector has been well documented as forced competition has led to intense pressure to adopt commercial models of strategy (i.e. based on competition).

The benefits of co-operative strategies from the data available so far indicate that they could become powerful programmes of strategic change for a range of organizations. Strategies generally take the form of joint ventures and alliances or agreements between different organizations to work together to attain some mutually desired strategic goal. They do not necessarily mean the demise of either of the partnership organizations as a separate entity, although in the extreme a full joint venture could bring with it the need to set up a new organization which embraced all the activities of the joint venture.

Until recently much information on alliances between organizations has been the professional preserve of financial specialists and corporate lawyers. However, this knowledge is now beginning to accumulate in management theory. It indicates that there would be benefits for many organizations which engaged in co-operative strategies. Drawing on the work of Byars (1984), Goldenberg (1988), Lynch (1989) and Lewis (1990), we could say that co-operative strategies could bring the following advantages and possibilities:

1 *The ability to think and act on a larger scale than ever before.* Organizations which collaborate enjoy economies of scale. For example, why limit the extent of service provision or product innovation to what the organization can do alone? The best alliance partners have what one organization has not (and vice versa). The result should be strategic synergy between organizational partners as they learn from each other.

2 *The facility to expand technological interdependence.* Expansion in the field of technology has been rapid. It has certainly outstripped the rate of economic growth to which most individual organizations are tied. In some areas (e.g. information technology) the pace of developments has often grown beyond the ability of the single organization to use them. Co-operation could allow organizations in any alliance to 'hybridize' and share the technological advantages between them.

3 *Reducing the risks and costs of innovation and development.* Large-scale projects can be shared between partners in the alliance. Again, this can be a process of expertise sharing. It can also be a factor in reducing overall administrative costs, since the alliance only requires one administrative support function. Similarly, the financial structure of project support can be immensely simplified between organizations in an alliance.

4 *Making the best use of management talent and expertise.* In situations where highly trained and expert managers are a scarce resource, alliances between organizations can allow existing levels of expertise to be shared around. It can also provide a forum for future management development strategies beyond the limitations of the current competence approaches (see previous section).

The precise form of co-operation can vary widely (see Byars 1984; Harrigan 1985). There can be 'spider's web' joint ventures in which a few large organizations and many small organizations co-operate in one service sector. The smaller organizations join in alliance with one or more of the larger organizations. Alternatively, alliances may be of the 'co-operate – then split' type, where organizations get together for a specific project which has a definite life span (e.g. a new building). Finally, the alliance may be based on 'successive integration'. Here organizations begin by co-operating at a distance in a weak joint venture. In time the alliance becomes stronger (and may result in merger, especially in the commercial sector).

One of the key consistent findings from all the empirical research on successful joint ventures is that they require delegation, responsible autonomy, internal co-operation from staff and high levels of commitment and loyalty at all levels. There is substantial evidence to show that joint ventures between organizations can bring with them immense benefits, ranging from the more effective use of resources and talents, greater ease of structural change and a firm basis for sustaining and supporting strategic change (Harrigan 1985).

ECONOMIC PROGRAMMES FOR CHANGE: DEREGULATION AND PRIVATIZATION

In virtually all economies under capitalism the propensity to create wealth through the accumulation of profit and increased levels of production produces its own form of 'crisis' (O'Connor 1973, 1974,

1984). This crisis is one in which there is a constant need to restructure both economic and social relations in the workplace. Put simply, the expansion of economies under capitalism cannot occur as a smooth process of growth. Rather, the contexts in which capital can be accumulated change as the markets they create take on their own dynamics of supply and demand. Thus change is something of a sporadic process. Under *laissez-faire* economic systems such crises occurred but there was no concerted attempt to direct the economy and to plan in advance the changes that accumulation crises brought about. During the last decade Britain (along with a number of other countries) has seen a concerted attempt to programme such economic changes so that profitable enterprise can continue and capital and wealth can accumulate. This planning of capitalist economies has brought into play a very particular form of programmed change. It may appear obscure, highly macro and irrelevant to the day-to-day management of change, yet it is ultimately the overall context in which organizations and their managers operate. It sets and determines the parameters within which they function, and in which all theories and models of change management are located.

The following analysis drawn from the British context is intended to be indicative rather than exhaustive. The changes described are those which are argued to be the major events which have fashioned the wider context. They also show the extent to which the wider socio-economic context has itself been managed, resulting in over a decade of constant change. The dynamics of change are, therefore both multivariate and occurring at many different levels of analysis. Whilst the wider socio-economic context was being steered in particular directions (particularly following the election of a Conservative government in 1979) managers had to translate, cope with and adapt to the changing conditions these events dictated. The model thus becomes one of change within change, rather than the management of organizational change *per se.*

The outcomes of economic changes since 1979 (although their origins pre-date the election of the conservative government) are threefold: (1) the decline of manufacturing industry and, hence, manufacturing employment levels, known popularly as deindustrialization, (2) transfer of ownership from public to private, coupled with a reduction in levels of public services, known popularly as privatization, (3) the massive increase in global markets, including the processes of 'Europeanization', industrialization of Third World countries, and the predominance of the multinational corporation.

The deregulation of many British industries such as tele-communications, power generation and other 'service' sectors, allowed the entry of competitors and the operation of free-market rules, often for the first time. The rules of the game became those of the 'enterprise culture' (see chapter 4), essentially a form of econ-omic Darwinism in which only the strong survive. Deregulation also occurred for the first time in the money markets with the deregul-ation of the British stock market.

In continental Europe and Britain there has been a constant shift towards a single European market in 1992. Trade and service industries have become more focused towards Europe (rather than towards North America). The demands this is beginning to place upon the language abilities of British managers (at least to speak some French and German) are noticeable. Traditional industrial relations, which dealt primarily with union–management negoti-ations, have taken a back seat for a while following the steady decline in the power of trade unions. The failure of union represen-tation in the civil service and the inability of the coal miners to achieve a stranglehold as tight as the one they had in 1973 are two examples. Others can be found in the printing industry as union resistance to the adoption of the new technology in newspaper production proved ineffective in stopping it from going ahead. Much managerial attention previously focused on union negotiations has been reallocated under the banner of human resource management.

Other changes have been in the rapid development and adoption of new technologies across a wide range of manufacturing and service organizations. In particular this includes the increasing use of computers, information systems, expert guidance systems for business decisions and for military operations (see Scarbrough and Corbett 1992 in this series). The disastrous results of alleged mis-management of technology can be seen in such large-scale disasters as those at Bhopal or Chernobyl. Another 'first' for the British finan-cial markets was the stock market crash in October 1987, referred to as 'Black Monday'.

These macro-economic changes have effects at the levels of the individual enterprise and the business sector. Financial institutions, for example, are having had to cope with massive changes in their environment. All have had to become more market-oriented, selling their services in competition with other financial institutions. This has meant severe 'downsizing' of the work force, with thousands of jobs being lost from the major clearing banks. Banks no longer need high-street presence, with lots of small retail outlets. For the corporate bank manager, recessions have forced a new attitude towards corporate lending (understanding the client's business) and business is currently very scarce.

The processes of deregulation and privatization have forced major changes on business sectors and individual managers. Some of the most important are those which allow private competition where none previously existed owing to a public company's protected monopoly rights. Key examples here are the 1980 Transport Act, which allowed competition on express coach routes, and the 1981 Telecommunications Act, which similarly allowed competition for British Telecom. The use of private contractors has meant that managers from the public sector are now having to manage the bidding process. Examples of this occur in the National Health Service, for catering and cleaning, and in the private provision of refuse collection services in a number of local authority areas (Hastings and Levie 1982: 12–14).

Europeanization will also create a very different context of change. Organizations which currently occupy a distinctive national niche will have to compete on the same terms as international traders. Levels of uncertainty will increase, since no one can predict the nature, scope and dynamics of the new markets. Wage rates and current bargaining practices are likely to change, and it is by no means clear which nations and industries will emerge as the leading players in the new game of Euro-economics. Some sectors, such as motor manufacture, will have to implement changes almost immediately. Other sectors, such as insurance, will have longer to plan and adapt. There is unlikely to be free trade in European insurance until 2001 at the earliest (*Economist*, July 1988). In this field, prices for premiums, scope for growth and regulations vary greatly between countries. Life policies cost three times as much in Italy as they do in England. Much variation is due to lack of competition within countries and the formation of large groups of cartels of insurance companies (Wilson and Rosenfeld 1990).

In a survey of twenty-six industrial sectors, (eighteen service and eight social service sectors) Sykes and Crabtree (1988) argue that questions of harmonizing investment policies, mergers and acquisitions, taxation, trade barriers and the level of public ownership of companies will have to be resolved. Maintaining a steady strategic course will be a major challenge for managers, since different specialisms in any organization will also face variation in demands upon their services in the new markets. Research and design, finance, marketing and technology-related specialisms are likely to become key functional areas.

This is particularly true in the context of the changes towards 'flexible specialization' (see Piore and Sabel 1984). Contextual changes have ensured that Taylorism and Fordism (see chapter 3) are no longer a firm basis for organization. Instead, the market demands the emergence of smaller-batch production, customized to client needs. Firms can achieve this with the support of technology in the guise of information systems, computerized design facilities and other microelectronic processes. As Zuboff (1988) notes, the power balance in such organizations is likely to shift towards those who understand and can use the new technology (a present-day equivalent of Pettigrew's 1973 empirical example of power where information proved to be the most potent power base).

SUMMARY

When discussing programmes of change it is important not to equate them solely with individual techniques for handling organizational change. The extent of programmes (and of programming) goes far beyond the reach of any individual strategies. From the level of analysis of the individual firm, it is obvious how the use of packages such as TQM will set the context in which future changes take place. Looking more broadly at industrial sectors reveals the strategic stereotyping that can cast a strong influence over the consideration of alternative strategies of change (see also chapter 5). At the national and international levels of analysis, it seems that the socio-economic context in which all organizations operate really sets the strategic agenda for change. Of course, this revisits the paradox of incrementalism. Whilst we may argue that the wider context determines everything we also have to consider how the prevailing strategies of the state came about. They, too, may have been the product of many smaller, more operational decisions which, when taken together, give the appearance of a large, global strategy. The study of programmatic approaches to strategic change, therefore, has to proceed with some care to avoid a seemingly inevitable logic of contextual determinism.

Chapter 7

A strategy of change: some conclusions

This book finds many of its origins in an immense dissatisfaction with the way in which theories of organizational change have, over time, become synonymous with the management of change. The former require a good appreciation of theories and competing frameworks for analysis. The latter requires a set of guidelines and principles for good management practice without the need of having to go through the bother of locating those terms within an analytical framework. The problem in merging theory and application is that many of the assumptions, biases and contradictions of the under-lying theories are lost in the haste to apply them. In much of the literature, and in many taught management courses, the manage-ment of change rather than the analysis of change has become the dominant factor.

This seems to be particularly the case at the individual level of analysis. Strategic change appears to be something which managers already excel at, or can be trained to handle. The management of change, therefore, was rapidly becoming just another skill to add to the managerial repertoire. This is not simply an 'academic' lament. Practitioners should be seriously worried too. The application of change recipes which have little empirical or theoretical foundation should give cause for grave concern amongst all who work in organ-izations of every type.

This is not to say that the theory and practice of change manage-ment are mutually exclusive. They are inextricably linked, since the one should inform the other. The problem seems to be that the practice of managing change (especially for individual managers) is becoming ever distant from the theories and knowledge which inform it. Change management has become something of 'a blue-print for action' (Plant 1987). Such blueprints were based on allegedly practical advice, couched in the emerging vocabulary of managerial good practice. This book is an attempt to revisit the theoretical terrain of organizational change and to place such recipe-driven models firmly in their context. Finally, the book will have succeeded (at least in my terms) if it causes readers to reflect upon whether the apparent answer to virtually all problems of organizational change is perhaps something other than 'change the culture to a project-based matrix, decentralize the organizational structure and bring in a change agent (preferably from a reputable firm of management consultants) to help the process along'.

A STRATEGY OF CHANGE: THE GAPS BETWEEN THEORY AND PRACTICE

As an intellectual investigation, understanding organizational change requires the appreciation of a vast network of competing theories, each drawn from many disciplines and perspectives. Some are covered in this book, although other areas of concern, such as morals and ethics, are not. No doubt other areas have been excluded or given only passing reference (as my intellectual peers will inform me). But the point of this book is that as a practical management guide all this change theory has a hard time in being convincing, especially to practising managers. In the realm of management education it seems to be those with the loudest voices who are assumed to have the route-to-the-truth in change management. This is particularly true of the vendors of recipes of best business practice. These are not just any vendors, either. Their credibility (to practising managers) comes from their having managed change themselves, or from being a respected 'guru', well informed in the art of managing change. In the course of time this process has led to a considerable level of homogeneity both in the appreciation of and in approaches to managing change.

Those authors who have sought to emphasize the complexity of change at the organizational and contextual levels (e.g. Pettigrew and Whipp 1991) have understandably been unable to match the seeming immediacy of the analyses of their more practical skills-oriented colleagues. Contextual analysis requires the careful and rigorous examination of antecedents, frames of reference, business sector characteristics – in short it needs to address both the archaeology and the genealogy of change. Brushing up one's interpersonal skills or individual decision style has the appearance of greater relevance and is, of course, far more tangible than asking awkward questions about the nature of change and the context in which it operates. Most books on individual change include questionnaires through which the readers can 'discover' their leadership style, appetite for working in groups, etc. In the extreme, this becomes just like reading one's horoscope – attractive at the level of individual curiosity but found wanting in the analytical progress it makes towards understanding the concept of change.

If organizations are to survive the immense pressures upon them, their managers need to be more than good operators at the level of individual skills. They need to understand the complexities of the processes and the nature of change in order to steer their organizations through the dynamics of change. This means perhaps revisiting the analysis of change, perhaps changing the ways in which academics disseminate the subject as management trainers and extending the analysis outside the relatively narrow confines of interpersonal and group analyses. This book has deliberately taken a particular stance toward the question of organizational change. The argument has been largely against skill-based approaches, ready-made models of good organizational practice (for example, the 'excellence' models) and reliance upon analysing change as primarily the outcome-oriented pursuit of great and charismatic individuals. The arguments have, rather, favoured the potency of organizational structures, of economic determinism, of institutionalization within which the manager must operate. To operate successfully (and in the long term) he or she must understand and learn from the wider context or organization. This is not to say that individual skills are unimportant, only that they cannot be considered in isolation from the wider factors of strategic change. Whether or not the reader agrees with such an analysis is not the point. It is the consideration of alternative views which promotes analysis, learning and the development of knowledge. The reader can then organize his or her own thoughts and come to a reasoned conclusion without over-dependence on readily accessible models and seemingly powerful metaphors.

IMPLICATIONS OF A MACRO-INTERDISCIPLINARY ANALYSIS OF CHANGE

Change is a phenomenon which cannot be restricted solely to the 'behavioural' aspects of management learning. It needs a perspective which can blend the behavioural with the economic, the historical with future-oriented decision-making, and the political with the social and economic factors of change. Unfortunately, current developments in the analysis of change have developed along the either/or path of skills versus context. For virtually every management discipline currently taught, the implications of this split are far-reaching.

Again, the implications extend beyond the academic to land squarely at the feet of the practitioner. Depending upon which perspective is taken, the practitioner will be guided or will turn towards a particular set of solutions to effect change. Consider, for example, the familiar problem in corporate strategy where the range of products and services offered by an organization does not align exactly with the vision of the strategic planners (or those responsible for planning). The pressure for change is acute, to try and change either the strategic plan or the range of products and services to achieve some state of congruence. On the one hand, one could argue that the solution for change might lie with the strategic planners, for it is they who have the 'vision'. Along the way, this vision may have become subject to the politics of organizational change, in which the smooth transition of stategic planning becomes clouded by internal politics and conflict or by fiscal and regulatory pressures in the operating environment of the organization. Thus those products or services which do emerge are unlikely to be in line with the vision of the strategic planners. Product and service range no longer match the articulated corporate strategy. The solution for change would thus be to keep the strategic vision constant, but try to reduce resistance and pressures from other sources during implementation. This could involve building teams in which planners and implementers worked together on the same problem, possibly in parallel teams (very like the Japanese process of new product development). Or it could involve negotiating directly or indirectly with those who resist the strategy, perhaps co-opting them into the early stages of product development. The change solution is likely to be rooted in behaviouralism, trying to persuade others to accept new ideas. Currently, this is akin to internal selling, which occurs in very decentralized firms or in organizations which are split up into strategic business units. New ideas generated by one part of the organization have to be 'sold' to other parts (e.g. development teams have to convince the marketing function that a proposed product will sell). The process of persuasion could take a number of forms.

Beyond co-optation, attention to management style, negotiating techniques and influencing skills might appear to be fruitful solutions to achieving change.

On the other hand, the solution for change might be found by analysing the political power balance in an organization (Hickson *et al.* 1986) rather than trying to persuade others to accept any pre-determined strategic plan. Here the analysis of change would be less overtly behavioural, taking the view that those products and services which do emerge are predominantly the result of the political inter-play of factions both inside and outside the organization. The solution for achieving change would appear to lie with the institutional features of organization, such as its structure, culture, context, technology or history. Increased persuasion by those who plan would seem pointless, since the organizational context will torpedo the vision. The key to handling strategic change is to understand the context and thus be able to predict the likely outcome of any action taken. Thus the system of organization itself allows change to take place, since understanding the process of strategic change through the institutionalized context allows variation and experimentation to take place. But it need not involve management development, the creation of teams, the decentralization of structures, the creation of strategic business units, or the intervention of an organizational development practitioner.

The above distinction is, however, only one dimension of a complex problem, even though, on this dimension alone, individuals would be tempted to take very different routes towards achieving change. What if the task were not just to align emergent outcomes with intended strategies, but was also to achieve greater innovation and creativity in products and services, something marketing analysts such as Kotler (1988) hold central to achieving competitive advantage? According to Etzioni (1988), reliance on strategic planning (held dear by neoclassical economists) can place limits on innovation and can ration creative effort by individuals throughout the organization. A range of products and services emerges, but they are characterized by their similarity to what went before. Alternatively, non-economic analyses which accord primacy to the emergent and processual aspects of organization mean that change processes increase the level of organizational politics, but decrease the amount of co-operation and co-ordination. Creativity and innovation might be fostered, but the range of products and services which do emerge is likely to be the outcome of intuitive or political decisions. They may or may not be successful in achieving and sustaining competitive advantage.

The implications for the 'management' of change are fundamental. The essential task is either to achieve greater creativity in formal strategic planning, or to abandon the idea of rational economic decisions altogether and instead focus attention upon analysing and managing the conflict and politics inside and outside the organization. But which way is the practitioner to jump? The current vogue for more behavioural solutions may be tempting, but are they likely to achieve strategic change in the long term? The answer from the available empirical evidence would seem to indicate that solutions based broadly upon behaviouralism and/or organizational development are relatively short-term. Those based upon more macro analyses of culture, structure and power are more difficult to achieve, but are more likely to be sustained in the longer term (Cummings and Huse 1989).

The reasons for this can be found in much earlier works (e.g. Blake and Mouton 1964). Achieving short-term change in behavioural aspects such as management style is relatively easy in comparison to making it a permanent feature of the organization. This is what Cummings and Huse (1989: 478) call 'institutionalizing an organization development intervention'. In other words, making it part of the organizational culture. The same authors note that, often, change efforts based on organization development become reliant on a single individual (the sponsor) and that when the sponsor leaves (or is transferred to a position of less influence or direct power) the programme of change collapses abruptly (p. 480). In Lewin's (1951) terms, there is an unfreezing, a change, but no refreezing of the new state.

The above would seem to advocate against using Organization Development techniques totally. That is not the intention. Organization Development is a valuable approach, provided it is viewed within the wider context of the organization. Too often, OD and other change programmes such as Quality of Working Life and Socio-Technical Systems have been seen as an end in themselves without reference to the context in which they operate. Both programmes make similar assumptions to more individually based intervention (such as changing management style). That is, increased worker autonomy and participation in work-related decisions leads to a more satisfied and therefore more productive work force. Like the other programmes for change described in chapter 6, they can also be beset with problems, proffer short term solutions, and can be viewed as a way of keeping workers happy by apparently democratizing the workplace but at the same time retaining ultimate managerial control. Yet some of the most carefully conducted experiments in organizational change also fall under the banner of OD.[1] Whilst the results of many studies are largely inconclusive, we should be careful not to dismiss such approaches too readily and should recognize that many alternative approaches to change (such as creating excellent cultures; designing matrix organizational structures) are likely to have even less empirical support and are unlikely to have been subjected to the same intellectual rigour in research design.

The search for more macro solutions to organizational change leads straight back to some of the ideas outlined at the beginning of this book. Fostering innovation in formal planning can be achieved by a number of apparently 'managed' routes. Where organizational structures are bureaucratic and hierarchical, for example, they can be decentralized, blurring the differentiation between functions and thus engaging individuals in the spirit of the whole enterprise rather than in just their part of it. Yet we know that purely structural solutions are unlikely to achieve this without the supporting ideologies (or cultures) in which organizational change and learning take place (Argyris 1977; Argyris and Schon 1978).

The amount of such institutional support that can be achieved may vary according to the amount of uncertainty facing the organization. The level of uncertainty can, itself, change with time, requiring organizations to develop different learning strategies. Drawing on the work of Argyris and Schon (1978), Butler (1991) distinguishes between inner-loop and outer-loop learning. Inner-loop learning takes place when organizations face a relatively stable and benign operating environment. Their macro context is stable. The prime goal of change becomes one of increasing efficiency. Outer-loop learning refers to changes which can no longer be handled by increasing efficiency but require deep, ideological changes to take place. The macro context is highly uncertain. It is worth noting at this stage that highly efficient organizations are only definable as such by their context. The term 'efficient' means they cope well with the current level of uncertainty in their operating environment. A major change in the operating environment means that such organizations can become progressively less effective and slide efficiently out of business if further learning does not take place. A macro analysis of change requires that the rate and level of change in the operating environment are monitored and counted in the overall equation.

In Britain, such an analysis reveals major changes in the operating context of virtually all organizations. There has been around a 33 per cent growth rate in service organizations between 1988 and 1990. In the same period, manufacturing organizations returned a 7.5 per cent growth (Central Statistical Office, January 1991). This has prompted many commentators to observe that Britain is in the process of change from a manufacturing to a predominantly service economy (Tailby and Whitston 1989). Such macro changes mean that if the philosophy is to replace manufacturing with a service economy, then strategies for change will differ, depending upon whether the firm is in manufacturing or services already. Compounded by a recessionary phase in the late 1980s and early 1990s, around 20,000 firms have folded, with the greatest number of victims in the manufacturing sector (although service organizations are also beginning to suffer). Survival would seem one obvious change strategy at this level of analysis.

Yet other common themes appear to emerge on a global scale among a mix of both manufacturing and service organizations. Britain may have its special problems in deciding the balance between manufacturing and services (compounded by the relative lack of availability of low-cost capital) but continental European and North American organizations share some striking similarities at the contextual level of analysis (Bartlett *et al.* 1990). These include acquisitions and joint ventures (single operators are beginning to recognize the limits to going it alone); the globalization of business (supported by the rationalization of production, improved quality, the adoption of new technology and marketing); the achievement of a strong corporate identity (occasionally termed culture) and the support for a strong research and development focus.

These macro-level changes will determine to a large extent the efficacy of more micro strategies of change (such as OD), since they will influence the extent to which behavioural and structural changes in work design can be sustained. Equally, programmes for change such as Total Quality, or Quality of Working Life, packages will be subject to the wider forces of determinism. Training managers to handle change through the learning of specific competences may achieve little more than enabling them to cope with change more easily (as opposed to being able to manage it). Joint ventures and acquisitions, for example, often involve organizations of very different cultures working together for the first time. Should the first step towards resolving the inevitable tension thus created be to try and create and manage a new superordinate culture? The excellence tradition would have us believe this is the first step, but empirical evidence weighs heavily against tackling corporate culture head-on (Cummings and Huse 1989).

The globalization of business brings with it similar problems. Organizations must seek some way of adapting to operating as global players, yet the impact of different national cultures and of economies which are in different stages of advance or decline will be major factors in the change equation (Tayeb 1989). Placing more emphasis on research and development will inevitably make these functions more 'strategically contingent' and allow them the potential to exert greater influence over strategic decisions, both in their planning and in their outcomes (Hickson *et al.* 1971, 1986). It is a debatable point whether other stakeholders in the organizations will let this change happen willingly. Wilson *et al.* (1986) provide empirical evidence of the inflexibility of organizations from both public and private sectors when a substantial shift in the power balance seems a likely outcome. Stakeholders defend their political position resolutely. This is what Wilson *et al.* (1986) term the 'bounding' of strategic decision-making. The institutionalized fabric of organizations resists change until something out of the ordinary happens. Four out-of-the-ordinary conditions are:

1   The advent of new data or technology in a form to which the organization is unaccustomed.
2   A significant increase in conflict between powerful stakeholders (both inside and outside the organization).
3   A novel topic for decision (i.e. one which the firm has never previously encountered in that form, although other firms may have taken similar decisions).
4   An unusual or unexpected source of new ideas which break through the traditional information channels and open up discussion.

Pettigrew (1985) adds the onset of crisis to the above list, arguing that a common perception among individuals that the organization is threatened with extinction also acts as a spur to 'unbound' the institutionalized context of the organization and overcome the inertia against change.

Yet the analysis of change can never be wholly deterministic, since, as we saw in chapter 2, change is itself a dynamic concept. The degree, scope, pace and immediacy of change will all influence the extent to which the management of change is a proactive or largely deterministic exercise. Scarbrough and Corbett (1992) illustrate this point with regard to the impact of new technologies and organizational design. Technology can be viewed as something 'neutral' which organizations choose to use or not. On the other hand, technology can be interpreted as both a social and a political force in the face of which organizations undergo often quite radical changes either to incorporate or to reject the 'new' technology.

This duality or dialectic is inherent in the study of organizational change. Its analysis gains potency from the tensions between voluntarism and determinism, and thus the knowledge base can be extended and developed. The danger lies in assuming change to be a simple phenomenon, attached as a sub-theme to organizational behaviour and manageable through a finite list of behavioural recipes and managerial competences. The study of organizational change requires an interdisciplinary focus which allows an appreciation of the contexts in which strategies for change are conceived and enacted. As empirical evidence grows, such a view is likely to gain greater support. Until that time it is to be hoped that the field of study does not fragment, or worse still, refuse itself to change from its current unsatisfactory position. This book does not pretend to give the answers, but makes a plea for a more general integration of approaches to the subject of organizational change, in particular not forgetting the intellectual traditions, contradictions and roots of analysis in our haste to try and solve the pressing problems of today's organizations.

This analysis comes down heavily in favour of a macro-contextual perspective. Programmes and packages, or individual 'blueprints for action' (Plant 1987) may appear appealing in their apparent scope and immediacy in stimulating action towards change. Yet all of them are bound in the wider contexts of organizational environments. The relevance and efficacy of programmes will be coloured by the context in which they are applied. Perhaps it is time for reflection and consideration, rather than pure application, which will ultimately lead towards a better understanding of the term 'a strategy of change'.

Notes

4 The process and implementation of strategic change

1 The sociology of power and particularly its relevance to complex organizations can be found in a wide range of literature. Some of the key debates can be found in Clegg (1974, 1979, 1990), Lukes (1974), Daudi (1986) and Pfeffer (1981). Essentially, the same frameworks of analysis that are used in the text here to examine change can be put to work in the analysis of power. There is a mainstream of theorizing, backed up by empirical evidence which examines power as a relational phenomenon in organizations. This perspective argues that power can be observed via the exercise of influence over overt decisions, for example. Those individuals, or parts of the organization, which are more 'powerful' than others gain their potency from the inequality of contingencies facing organizations. Power accrues to those who can handle the inherent uncertainty created by these contingencies. On the other hand, power can be viewed through the conceptual lens of agenda setting and manipulation. Strategic choices which are not open to the influence of individuals and groups tell us much about the power of those who keep such issues away from the formal agenda. Power has also been subjected to deconstruction, to the extent that Daudi (1986: 266) states, 'Really one could say that power, as such, does not exist. The concept seems to be used to denote "existing" mechanisms in society. Power may be seen as an immanent phenomenon in social relations between groups and individuals.' The logical fallacy of this argument *in extremis* is that analysis cannot be aimed at something which does not exist, since we impute power from social interaction. Yet to study power, Daudi argues, we should study and observe social action. The same debates, of course, can be applied to the concept of strategic change, but in that case there are at least two different 'existences' before and after change. I suspect that even the most extreme form of reductionism in the study of change would result in the study of social action or individuals' accounts of their own actions and those of others. It is here that the study of strategic change diverges from the study of power. At best, the analysis of power can yield only a partial explanation of the phenomenon of change.

2   Adapted from the *Guardian*, 23 January 1991, p. 21.

3   The last decade has seen an enormous increase in critical thinking and theorizing in financial disciplines. For those interested in the details of the debates as they relate both to understanding the epistemology of accounting and to the processes of strategic change, the work of Richard Laughlin and Anthony Lowe at the School of Management and Economic Studies, University of Sheffield, is a well argued position statement. See also writings by Brendan McSweeney and Keith Hoskin at the University of Warwick Business School, and those of Anthony Hopwood at the London School of Economics.

5 Organizational culture and change

1   I am indebted to my colleague Sebastian Green, who first alerted me to this analysis whilst he was at the London Business School in the late 1980s. We had both travelled to Warwick by train from London and a breakdown on the return journey gave us ample time to discuss points of mutual interest. The analysis is deeply rooted in the theatre and in the consideration of history and language. Sebastian Green is the first person I encountered who took the work of writers such as Wendy Griswold from studies of the theatre and applied its ideas directly to a critique of organizational culture.

2   The national culture debates continue as conflicting research evidence accumulates. A dominant approach to classifying national cultures is to search for broad differences in the attitudes and values of individuals and then to create a taxonomy of national differences. The work of Hofstede and Tayeb is typical of this approach. As the process of scientific enquiry progresses, critiques are beginning to emerge, one of which is due to appear later in this series (jointly authored by David Cray and Geoff Mallory).

3   Hofstede's work is summarized here in four clusters of countries. In the original, at least six clusters can be identified, using other factors. The four used in this chapter, however, represent the main factors in the research as well as those which present the most clear-cut results.

6 Programmed approaches to organizational change

1   The impact of co-operative strategies is likely to become the focus of much substantial and important research in the 1990s and beyond. Across a wide range of organizations, governments and whole economies, the disadvantages of competition as a dominant strategy are beginning to force co-operation. This will have immense implications for managing co-operation, for managing the change from competition to co-operation, for understanding the dynamic forces which sustain co-operative alliances, and for developing and building theories which can guide and predict the characteristics and outcomes of strategic alliances of all kinds. Work in this area is beginning at the Centre for Corporate Strategy and Change at the University of Warwick under the direction of Professor Andrew Pettigrew. Other major research centres of

management and organizations, economics and politics are also beginning to turn their attention to researching co-operative strategies.

7 A strategy of change: some conclusions

1   Socio-Technical theories date back to the early 1950s, when, in early experiments in coal mines, chemical, textile and paper producing factories, it was discovered that absenteeism was significantly reduced and productivity significantly increased when work design was shaped by the consideration of both technological and social factors (Trist and Bamforth 1951; Rice 1958; Emery and Trist 1960a,b). From these and other related studies the Quality of Working Life movement was generated. It combined social concerns (the well-being of staff) with those of organizational effectiveness. Participative problem-solving, redesigning jobs, quality circles, improving reward systems and introducing flexible working hours are all commonly known aspects of QWL programmes (Walton 1974; Taylor 1977; Gyllenhammer 1977; Steel and Shane 1986).

References

Adorno, T. W. (1973) *The Jargon of Authenticity*, London: Routledge.

Alderfer, C. (1977) 'Organization development', in M. R. Rozenweig and L. W. Porter (eds) *Annual Review of Psychology* 28, 2:197–223.

Aldrich, H. E. (1971) *Organizations and Environments*, Englewood Cliffs, N.J.: Prentice-Hall.

Aldrich, H. E. (1979), *Organizations and Environments*, Eaglewood Cliffs, N.J.: Prentice Hall.

Aldrich, H. E., in collaboration with E. Auster, U. Staber and C. Zimmer (1986) *Population Perspectives on Organizations*, Uppsala: Acta Universitatis Upsaliensis.

Argyris, C. (1977) 'Organizational learning and management information systems', *Accounting, Organizations and Society* 2, 2:113–29.

Argyris, C., and Schon, D. A. (1978) *Organizational Learning: Theory of Action Perspective*, Reading, Mass.: Addison-Wesley.

Armstrong, P. (1989) 'Limits and possibilities for HRM in an age of management accountancy', in J. Storey (ed.) *New Perspectives on Human Resource Management*, London: Routledge.

Asch, S. E. (1955) 'Studies of independence and conformity: a minority of one against unanimous majority', *Psychological Monographs* 20 (whole No. 416).

Atkinson, J. (1984) 'Manpower strategies for flexible organizations', *Personnel Management*, August: 23–7.

Bachrach, P., and Baratz, M. S. (1970) *Power and Poverty: Theory and Practice*, London: Oxford University Press.

Barker, D. L., and Allen, S. (eds) (1976) *Dependence and Exploitation in Work and Marriage*, London: Longman.

Barlow, G. (1989) 'Deficiencies and the perpetuation of power: latent functions in management appraisal', *Journal of Management Studies* 26, 5:499–517.

Bartlett, C., Doz, Y., and Hedlund, G. (eds) (1990) *Managing the Global Firm*, London: Routledge.

Bedeian, H. (1987) 'Organization theory: current controversies, issues and directions', in C. L. Cooper and I. T. Robertson (eds) *International Review of Industrial and Organizational Psychology*, New York: Wiley.

Benson, J. K. (1975) ' The interorganizational network as a political economy', *Administrative Science Quarterly* 20, 3:229–49.

Benson, J. K. (1977) 'Organizations: a dialectical view', *Administrative Science Quarterly* 22, 1:1–21.

Bettis, R. A. and Donaldson, L. (1990) 'Market discipline and the discipline of management', *Academy of Management Review* 15, 3:367–8.

Blake, R. R. and Mouton, J. S. (1964) *The Managerial Grid*, Houston, Tx.: Gulf.

Blau, P., and Schoenherr, R. (1971) *The Structure of Organizations*, New York: Basic Books.

Braverman, H. (1974) *Labour and Monopoly Capitalism: the Degradation of Work in the Twentieth Century*, New York: Monthly Review Press.

Braybrooke, D. and Lindblom, C. E. (1963) *A Strategy of Decision*, New York: Free Press.

Brorverman, I. K. (1972) 'Sex role stereotypes: a current appraisal', *Journal of Social Issues* 28, 1:59–78.

Bryman, A. (1986) *Leadership and Organizations*, London: Routledge.

Burawoy, M. (1985) *The Politics of Production: Factory Regimes under Capitalism and Socialism*, London: Verso.

Burchell, S., Clubb, C., Hopwood, A., Hughes, J., and Nahapiet, J. (1980) 'The role of accounting in organizations and society', *Accounting, Organizations and Society* 5, 1:5–27.

Burns, T., and Stalker, G. M. (1961) *The Management of Innovation*, London: Tavistock.

Burrell, G. (1984) 'Sex and organizational analysis', *Organization Studies* 5, 2:97–118.

Burrell, G. (1991) 'A review of Alex Stewart, *Team Entrepreneurship*', *Organization Studies* 12, 1:144–5.

Burrell, G., and Morgan, G. (1979) *Sociological Paradigms and Organizational Analysis*, London: Heinemann.

Butler, R. J. (1991) *Designing Organizations: a Decision Making Perspective*, London: Routledge.

Butler, R. J., and Wilson, D. C. (1990) *Managing Voluntary and Non-profit Organizations: Strategy and Structure*, London: Routledge.

Byars, L. L. (1984) *Concepts of Strategic Management: Planning and Implementation*, New York: Harper & Row.

Calori, R., and Sarnin, P. (1991) 'Corporate culture and economic performance: a French study', *Organization Studies* 12, 1:49–74.

Child, J. (1972) 'Organizational structure, environment and performance: the role of strategic choice', *Sociology* 6, 1:1–22.

Clegg, S. (1974) *Power, Rule and Domination*, London: Routledge.

Clegg, S. (1979) *The Theory of Power and Organization*, London: Routledge.

Clegg, S. (1990) *Frameworks of Power*, London: Sage.

Clegg, S., and Dunkerley, D. (1977) *Critical Issues in Organizations*, London: Routledge.

Clegg, S., and Dunkerley, D. (1980) *Organization, Class and Control*, London: Routledge.

Cohen, M. D., March, J. G., and Olsen, J. P. (1972) 'A garbage can model of organizational choice', *Administrative Science Quarterly* 17, 1:1–25.

Constable, R., and McCormick, R. J. (1987) *The Making of British Managers: a Report for the BIM and CBI into Management Training, Education and Development*, London: BIM.

Cooley, M. J. E. (1987) *Architect or Bee? The Human Price of Technology*, London: Hogarth Press.

Crozier, M. (1964) *The Bureaucratic Phenomenon*, London: Tavistock.

Cummings, T. G., and Huse, E. F. (1989) *Organization Development and Change*, 4th edition, New York: West.

Cyert, R. M., and March, J. G. (1963) *A Behavioural Theory of the Firm*, Englewood Cliffs, N.J.: Prentice-Hall.

Daudi, P. (1986) *Power in the Organization: the Discourse of Power in Managerial Praxis*, Oxford: Blackwell.

Delamarter, R. T. (1988) *Big Blue: IBM's Use and Abuse of Power*, London: Pan.

Deming, W. E. (1986) *Out of the Crisis*, Cambridge, Mass.: MIT Center for Advanced Engineering Study.

Demski, J. S. (1972) *Information Analysis*, New York: Addison-Wesley.

Denison, D. R. (1984) 'Bringing corporate culture to the bottom line', *Organizational Dynamics*, autumn: 5–22.

Denison, D. R. (1990) *Corporate Culture and Organizational Effectiveness*, New York: Wiley.

Department of Health (1988) *Women Doctors and their Careers: Report of the Joint Working Party*, Heywood, Lancs.: Department of Health Publications.

Di Maggio, P., and Powell, W. (1983) 'The iron cage revisited: institutional isomorphism and collective rationality in organizational fields', *American Sociological Review*, 48, 147–60.

Dunford, R. (1990) 'A reply to Dunphy and Stace', *Organization Studies* 11, 1:131–5.

Dunphy, D. C., and Stace, D. A. (1988) 'Transformational and coercive strategies for planned organizational change', *Organizational Studies* 9, 3:317–34.

Emery, F. E., and Trist, E. L. (1960a) 'Socio-Technical Systems', in C. W. Churchman and M. Verhulst (eds) *Management Science, Models and Techniques*, London: Pergamon.

Emery, F. E., and Trist, E. L. (1960b) 'Socio-technical Systems', in *Management Sciences Models and Techniques* 2, London: Pergamon.

Etzioni, A. (1988) *The Moral Dimension: Toward a New Economics*, New York: Free Press.

Evan, W. M. (1971) 'The organizational set: toward a theory of interorganizational relations', in J. D. Thompson (ed.) *Approaches to Organizational Design*, Pittsburgh, Pa.: Pittsburgh University Press.

Feldman, S. P. (1989) 'The broken wheel: the inseparability of autonomy and control in innovation within the organization', *Journal of Management Studies* 26, 2:83–102.

Fombrun, C., and Shanley, M. (1990) 'What's in a name? Reputation building and corporate strategy', *Academy of Management Journal* 33, 2:233–58.

Foucault, M. (1973) *The Order of Things: an Archaeology of the Human Sciences*, New York: Vintage Books.

Gardiner, J. (1976) 'Political economy of domestic labour in capitalist society', in D. L. Barker and S. Allen (eds) *Dependence and Exploitation in Work and Marriage*, London: Longman.

Garfinkel, H. (1967) *Studies in Ethnomethodology*, New York: Prentice-Hall.

Gerson, E. M. (1976) 'On quality of life', *American Sociological Review* 41, October: 793–806.

Gioia, D. A. and Pitre, E. (1990) 'Multiparadigm perspectives on theory building', *Academy of Management Review* 15, 4:584–602.

Goffman, E. (1982) *The Presentation of Self in Everyday Life*, London: Pelican.

Goldenberg, S. (1988) *International Joint Ventures in Action*, London: Hutchinson.

Gouldner, A. (1980) *The Two Marxisms*, London: Macmillan.

Greenwood, R., and Hinings, C. R. (1988) 'Organizational design types, tracks and the dynamics of strategic change', *Organization Studies* 9, 3:293–316.

Greiner, L. (1972) 'Evolution and revolution as organizations grow', *Harvard Business Review* 50: July–August: 37–46.

Grinyer, P. H. and Spender, J. C. (1979) 'Recipes, crises and adaptation in mature businesses', *International Studies of Management and Organization* 9, 3:113–23.

Grinyer, P. H., Mayes, D., and McKiernan, P. (1987) *Sharpbenders: the Secrets of Unleashing Corporate Potential*, Oxford: Blackwell.

Gyllenhammer, P. (1977) *People at Work*, Reading, Mass.: Addison-Wesley.

Hallet Carr, E. (1961) *What is History? The George Macaulay Trevelyan Lectures delivered at the University of Cambridge*, New York: Vintage Books.

Handy, C. B. (1986) *Understanding Organizations*, Harmondsworth: Penguin.

Handy, C. B. (1987) *The Making of Managers*, London: NEDO.

Harrigan, K. R. (1985) *Strategies for Joint Ventures*, New York: D. C. Heath, Lexington Books.

Harrigan, K. R. (1986) *Managing for Joint Venture Success*, New York: D. C. Heath, Lexington Books.

Harrigan, K. R. (1987) 'Joint ventures: creating strategic change', in A. M. Pettigrew (ed.) *The Management of Strategic Change*, Oxford: Blackwell.

Hastings, S., and Levie, H. (eds) (1982) *Privatization?* Nottingham, Spokesman.

Hawley, A. H. (1950) *Human Ecology: a Theory of Community Structure*, New York: Ronald Press.

Hayes, C., Anderson, A., and Fonda, N. (1984) *Competence and Competition: Training and Education in the Federal Republic of Germany, the United States and Japan*, London: NEDO/MSC.

Hearn, J., and Parkin, P. W. (1983) 'Gender and organizations: a selective review and a critique of a neglected area', *Organization Studies* 4, 3:219–42.

Hedberg, B. (1981) 'How organizations learn and unlearn', in P. Nystrom and W. Starbuck (eds) *Handbook of Organizational Design* 1:3–27, Oxford: Oxford University Press.

Hickson, D. J., Butler, R. J., Cray, D., Mallory, G., and Wilson, D. C. (1986)

Top Decisions: Strategic Decision Making in Organizations, Oxford: Blackwell; San Francisco: Jossey-Bass.

Hickson, D. J., Hinings, C. R., Lee, C. A., Schneck, R. E., and Pennings, J. M. (1971) 'A strategic contingencies theory of intraorganizational power', *Administrative Science Quarterly* 16, 2:216–29.

Hinings, C. R., Hickson, D. J., Pennings, J. M., and Schneck, R. E. (1974) 'Structural conditions of intraorganizational power', *Administrative Science Quarterly* 19, 1:22–44.

Hofstede, G. (1980) *Culture's Consequences: International Differences in Work-related Values*, London and Beverly Hills: Sage.

Hofstede, G. (1990) 'The cultural relativity of organizational practices and theories', in D. C. Wilson and R. H. Rosenfeld, *Managing Organizations: Text, Readings and Cases*, McGraw-Hill: London.

Hopwood, A. G. (1978) 'Towards an organizational perspective for the study of accounting and information systems', *Accounting, Organizations and Society* 4, 2:145–7.

Hopwood, A. G. (1983) 'On trying to study accounting in the contexts in which it operates', *Accounting, Organizations and Society* 8:287–305.

Hosking, D. M. (1988) 'Organizing, leadership, and skilful processes', *Journal of Management Studies* 25, 2:147–66.

Hosking, D. M. (1990) 'Leadership processes: the skills of political decision-making', in D. C. Wilson and R. H. Rosenfeld, *Managing Organizations: Text, Readings and Cases*, London: McGraw-Hill.

House, R. J. (1971) 'A path–goal theory of leader effectiveness', *Administrative Sciences Quarterly* 16, 3:321–38.

Hughes, M. (1985) 'Debureaucratization and private interest government: the British state and economic development policy', in W. Streeck and P. C. Schmitter (eds) *Private Interest Government: beyond Market and State*, London: Sage.

Isabella, L. A. (1990) 'Evolving interpretations as a change unfolds: how managers construe key organizational events', *Academy of Management Journal* 33, 1:7–41.

Jaedicke, R. K., and Robichek, A. A. (1964) 'Cost–volume–profit analysis under conditions of uncertainty', *Accounting Review* 39, 4:917–26.

Janis, I. L. (1972) *Victims of Groupthink: a Psychological Study of Foreign Policy Decisions and Fiascos*, Boston, Mass.: Houghton Mifflin.

Jessop, B., *et al.* (1988) *Thatcherism*, Oxford: Polity Press.

Johnson, G. (1987) *Strategic Change and the Management Process*, Oxford: Blackwell.

Johnson, G., and Scholes, K. (1988) *Exploring Corporate Strategy*, Englewood Cliffs, N.J.: Prentice-Hall.

Kahn, R. L. (1974) 'Organization development: some problems and proposals', *Journal of Applied Behavioral Science* 10, 4:485–502.

Kanter, R. M. (1977) *Men and Women of the Corporation*, New York: Basic Books.

Kanter, R. M. (1983) *The Change Masters: Corporate Entrepreneurs at Work*, New York: Counterpoint.

Kanter, R. M. (1989) *When Giants Learn to Dance*, New York: Irwin.

Keat, R., and Abercrombie, N. (eds) (1990) *Enterprise Culture*, London: Routledge.

Keep, E. (1989) 'A training scandal', in K. Sisson (ed.) *Personnel Management in Britain*, Oxford: Blackwell.

Kimberly, J. R., and Miles, R. H. and associates (1980) *The Organizational Life-cycle*, San Francisco: Jossey-Bass.

Kinch, N. (1988) *Strategic Illusion as a Management Strategy: the Volvo Story in Retrospect*, Working Paper Series 2, Department of Business Administration, University of Uppsala.

Kotler, P. (1988) *Marketing Management: Analysis, Planning Implementation and Control*, 6th edition, Englewood Cliffs, N.J.: Prentice-Hall.

Kotter, J. P., Schlesinger, L. A., and Sathe, V. (eds) (1986) *Organization: Text, Cases and Readings on the Management of Organizational Design and Change*, Homewood, Ill.: Irwin.

Lammers, C. J. (1990) 'Sociology of organizations around the globe', *Organization Studies* 11, 2:179–205.

Lammers, C. J., and Hickson, D. J. (eds) (1979) *Organizations Alike and Unlike*, London: Routledge.

Lawrence, P. R., and Lorsch, J. R. (1967) *Organization and Environment*, Cambridge Mass.: Harvard University Press.

Leavitt, H. J. (1972) *Managerial Psychology*, second edition, Chicago: University of Chicago Press.

Leavitt, H. J. (1991) 'A survey of management education', *Economist*, 2–8 March: 1–28.

Lewin, K. (1951) *Field Theory in Social Science*, New York: Harper & Row.

Lewis, J. D. (1990) *Partnerships for Profit: Structuring and Managing Strategic Alliances*, New York: Free Press.

Lindblom, C. E. (1959) 'The science of muddling through', *Public Administration Review* XIX, 2:79–88.

Lowe, E. A., and Shaw, R. W. (1968) 'An analysis of managerial biasing: evidence from a company's budgeting process', *Journal of Management Studies* 5, 4:304–15.

Lowin, A., Hottes, J. H., Sandler, B. E. and Bornstein, M. (1971) 'The pace of life and sensitivity to time in urban and rural settings: a preliminary study', *Journal of Social Psychology* 83, 3:247–53.

Lukes, S. (1974) *Power: a Radical View*, London: Macmillan.

Lynch, R. P. (1989) *The Practical Guide to Joint Ventures and Corporate Alliances: How to Form, How to Organize, How to Operate*, New York: Wiley.

Lynne, R. (1966) 'Brainwashing techniques in leadership and child-rearing', *British Journal of Social and Clinical Psychology* 5, 3:270–3.

Malinowski, B. (1945). *The Dynamics of Culture Change*, New Haven, Conn.: Yale University Press.

Mangham, I. L. (1986) *Power and Performance in Organizations: an Exploration of Executive Process*, Oxford: Blackwell.

Mangham, I. L., and Silver, M. S. (1986) *Management Training: Context and Practice*, London: Economic and Social Research Council.

Mansfield, R. (1990) 'Conceptualizing and managing the organizational environment', in D. C. Wilson and R. H. Rosenfeld (1990), *Managing Organizations: Text, Readings and Cases*, London: McGraw-Hill.

March, J. G., and Olsen, J. P. (1976) *Ambiguity and Choice in Organizations*, Bergen: Universitetsforlaget.

March, J. G., and Simon, H. A. (1958) *Organizations*, New York: Wiley.

Martin, C. J., and Clarke, B. A. (1990) 'Executive information systems: recent developments and research imperatives', *British Journal of Management* 1, 1:27–34.

McKiernan, P. (1992) *Strategies of Growth: Maturity, Recovery and Internationalization*, London: Routledge.

Meier, R. L. (1962) *A Communications Theory of Urban Growth*, Cambridge, Mass.: MIT Press.

Meier, R. L. (1968) 'The metropolis as a transaction maximizing system', *Daedulus* 97, 4:110–28.

Meyer, J. M., and Rowan, B. (1977) 'Institutionalized organization: formal structures as myth and ceremony', *American Journal of Sociology* 83, 2:340–63.

Meyer, M. W., and Zucker, L. G. (1989) *Permanently Failing Organizations*, Beverly Hills, Cal.: Sage.

Miles, R. E. and Snow, C. C. (1984) 'Fit, failure and the hall of fame,' *California Management Review* 26, 3:10–28.

Miller, D. and Friesen, P. H. (1984) *Organizations: a Quantum View*, New York: Prentice-Hall.

Mills, A. (1988) 'Organization, gender and culture', *Organization Studies* 9, 3:351–69.

Mintzberg, H. (1973) *The Nature of Managerial Work*, New York: Harper & Row.

Mitroff, I. I., and Kilmann, R. H. (1976) 'On organization stories: an approach to the design and analysis of organizations through myths and stories', in R. H. Kilmann, L. R. Pondy and D. P. Slevin (eds.) *The Management of Organization Design: Strategies and Implementation*, New York: North Holland.

Morgan, G. (1989) *Riding the Waves of Change*, London: Sage.

Nichols, T., and Beynon, H. (1977) *Living with Capitalism*, London: Routledge.

Norris, C. (1987) *Derrida*, London: Fontana.

Oakland, J. (1989) *Total Quality Management*, London: Heinemann.

O'Connor, J. (1973) *The Fiscal Crisis of the State*, New York: St. Martin's Press.

O'Connor, J. (1974) *The Corporations and the State*, New York: St Martin's Press.

O'Connor, J. (1984) *Accumulation Crisis*, Oxford: Blackwell.

Offe, C. (1976) *Industry and Inequality*, London: Arnold.

Otley, D. T. (1980) 'The contingency theory of management accounting: achievement and prognosis', *Accounting, Organizations and Society* 5, 4:413–28.

Otley, D. T. (1984) *Management Accounting and Organization Theory: a review of their interrelationship*, London: Macmillan-ESRC.

Peters, T. (1987) *Thriving on Chaos*, London: Pan.

Peters, T., and Austin, N. (1985) *A Passion for Excellence: the Leadership Difference*, London: Guild.

Peters, T., and Waterman, R., jr. (1982) *In Search of Excellence: Lessons from America's Best-run Companies*, New York: Harper & Row.

Pettigrew, A. M. (1973) *The Politics of Organizational Decision-making*, London: Tavistock.

Pettigrew, A. M. (1979) 'On studying organizational cultures', *Administrative Science Quarterly* 24, 4:570–81.

Pettigrew, A. M. (1985) *The Awakening Giant: Continuity and Change in ICI*, Oxford: Blackwell.

Pettigrew, A. M. (1990a) 'Longitudinal field research on change: theory and practice', *Organizational Science* 3, 1:120–38.

Pettigrew, A. M. (1990b) 'Studying strategic choice and strategic change: a comment on Mintzberg and Waters, "Does decision get in the way?"', *Organization Studies* 11, 1:6–11.

Pettigrew, A. M. (1990c) 'Is corporate culture manageable?' in D. C. Wilson and R. H. Rosenfeld, *Managing Organizations: Text, Readings and Cases*, London: McGraw-Hill.

Pettigrew, A. M., and Whipp, R. (1991), *Managing Change for Competitive Success*, Oxford: Blackwell.

Pettigrew, A. M., Whipp, R., and Rosenfeld, R. H. (1989) 'Competitiveness and the management of strategic change processes', in A. Francis and P. K. M. Tharakan (eds) *The Competitiveness of European Industry*, London: Routledge.

Pfeffer, J. (1981) *Power in Organizations*, London: Pitman.

Piore, M., and Sabel, C. F. (1984) *The Second Industrial Divide: Possibilities of Prosperity*, New York: Basic Books.

Plant, R. (1987) *Managing Change and Making it Stick*, London: Fontana.

Pollert, A. (1981) *Girls, Wives, Factory Lives*, London: Macmillan.

Porter, M. E. (1980) *Competitive Strategy*, New York: Free Press.

Quinn, J. B. (1980) *Strategies for Change: Logical Incrementalism*, New York: Irwin.

Quinn, R. E., and Kimberly, J. R. (1984) 'Paradox, planning and perseverance: guidelines for managerial practice', in J. Kimberly and R. Quinn (eds) *New Futures: the Challenge of Managing Organizational Transitions*, Ill.: Dow Jones–Irwin Homewood.

Quinn, R. E., Faerman, S. R., Thompson, M. P., and McGrath, M. R. (1990) *Becoming a Master Manager: a Competency Framework*, New York: Wiley.

Reed, M. (1985) *Redirections in Organizational Analysis*, London: Tavistock.

Rice, A. (1958) *Productivity and Social Organization: the Ahmedabad Experiment*, London: Tavistock.

Riley, P. (1983) 'A structurationist account of political culture', *Administrative Science Quarterly* 28, 1:30–45.

Risto, H. (1990) 'Sociology as a discursive space – the coming age of a new orthodoxy?', *Acta Sociologica* 33, 4:305–20.

Roberts, J. and Scapens, R. W. (1985) 'Accounting systems and systems of accountability – understanding accounting practices in their organizational contexts', *Accounting, Organizations and Society* 10, 4:443–56.

Rosen, B., and Jerdee, T. H. (1974) 'Influence of sex role stereotypes on personnel decisions', *Journal of Applied Psychology* 59, 1:9–14.

Sadler, P. (1989) 'Management development', in K. Sisson (ed.) *Personnel Management in Britain*, Oxford: Blackwell.

Salaman, G. (1981) *Classes and the Corporation*, London: Fontana.

Scarbrough, H., and Corbett, J. M. (1992) *Technology and Organization: Power, Meaning and Design*, London: Routledge.

Schein, E. H. (1984) 'Coming to a new awareness of organizational culture', *Sloan Management Review* 25, 1:3–16.

Schein, E. H. (1986) *Organizational Culture and Leadership*, San Francisco: Jossey-Bass.

Scherkenbach, W. W. (1988) *The Deming Route to Quality and Productivity*, Rockville, Md.: CEEP Mercury Press, George Washington University.

Schiff, M., and Lewin, A. Y. (1970) 'The impact of people on budgets', *Accounting Review*. 45, 2:259–68.

Shaw, J. (1976) 'Finishing school: some implications of sex-segregated education', in D. L. Barker and S. Allen (eds) *Sexual Divisions and Society: Process and Change*, London: Tavistock.

Silver, M. (1987) 'The ideology of excellence: management and neo-conservatism', *Studies in Political Economy* 24, 1:105–29.

Silverman, D. (1970) *Theories of Organizations*, London: Heinemann.

Skinner, B. F. (1961) *Analysis of Behavior*, London and New York: McGraw-Hill.

Smircich, L., and Stubbart, C. (1985) 'Strategic management in an enacted environment', *Academy of Management Review* 10, 4:724–36.

Snow, C. C., and Hrebiniak, L. G. (1983) 'Strategy, distinctive competence and organizational performance', *Administrative Science Quarterly* 25, 3:317–35.

Steel, R., and Shane, G. (1986) 'Evaluation research on quality circles: technical and analytical implications', *Human relations* 39:449–68.

Storey, J., and Sisson, K. (1989) 'Looking to the future', in J. Storey (ed.) *New Perspectives on Human Resource Management*, London: Routledge.

Strauss, G. (1976) 'Organization development', in R. Dubin (ed.) *Handbook of Work, Organization and Society*, Chicago: Rand McNally.

Sudnow, D. (1967) *Passing on: the Social Psychology of Dying*, New York: Prentice-Hall.

Sykes, D., and Crabtree, C. (eds) (1988) *Towards 1992*, University of Warwick Business Information Service, Warwick Research Institute.

Tailby, S., and Whitston, C. (eds.) (1989) *Manufacturing Change: Industrial Relations and Restructuring*, Oxford: Blackwell.

Tasini, J. (1991) 'Troubles in Toyland', *Best of Business International*, winter 1990/1:68–70.

Tayeb, M. (1989) *Organizations and National Culture: a Comparative Analysis*, London: Sage.

Taylor, F. W. (1911) *The Principles of Scientific Management*, New York: Harper.

Taylor, J. (1977) 'Job satisfaction and quality of working life', *Journal of Occupational Psychology* 50, 2:243–52.

Thomas, K. W. (1977) 'Toward multidimensional values in teaching: the example of conflict behaviours', *Academy of Management Review*, July: 472–91.

Thompson, P., and McHugh, D. (1990) *Work Organisations: a Critical Introduction*, London: Macmillan.

Thorne, P. (1991) *Mastering Change Management*, London: McGraw-Hill.

Trist, E. L., and Bamforth, K. W. (1951) 'Some social and psychological consequences of the long-wall method of coal getting', *Human Relations* 4, 1:3–38.

Turner, B. (1986) 'Sociological aspects of organizational symbolism', *Organization Studies* 7, 1:101–15.

Von Bertalanffy, L. (1956) 'General systems theory', in *General Systems: Yearbook of the Society for the Advancement of General Systems Theory* 1:1–10.

Vroom, V. H., and Yetton, P. (1973) *Leadership and Decision Making*, Pittsburgh, Pa.: University of Pittsburgh Press.

Walker, C. R. and Guest, R. H. (1952) *The Man on the Assembly Line*, Cambridge, Mass.: Harvard University Press.

Walsh, J. (1989) 'Capital restructuring and technological change: a case study of a British textile multinational', in S. Tailby and C. Whitston (eds) *Manufacturing Change: Industrial Relations and Restructuring*, Oxford: Blackwell.

Walton, R. (1974) 'Improving the quality of work life', *Harvard Business Review* 52, 1:20–5.

Watzke, G. E. (1971) 'Pace of Life as an Environmental Influence upon Organizations', Ph.D. dissertation, University Graduate School of Business, Stanford, Cal.

Watzke, G. E. (1972) *Pace in Organizations and the Community Pace of Life*, Preprint Series, Berlin: International Institute of Management.

Whipp, R. (1988) 'A time to every purpose: an essay on time and work,' in P. Joyce (ed.) *The Historical Meanings of Work*, Cambridge: Cambridge University Press.

Whipp, R., and Clark, P. (1986) *Innovation and the Auto Industry: Product, Process and Work Organization*, London: Pinter.

Weick, K. (1979) *The Social Psychology of Organizing*, Reading, Mass.: Addison–Wesley.

Wicks, J. (1988) 'Fritz Fahrini sees chances and changes for Sulzer', *Swiss Business*, September: 6–12.

Wildavsky, A. (1979) *The Politics of the Budgeting Process*, Boston, Mass.: Little Brown.

Wilk, J. (1990) 'Some Common Myths about Change', paper presented to the British Academy of Management Annual Conference, Glasgow University, September.

Williamson, O. E. (1975) *Markets and Hierarchies: Analysis and Antitrust Implications*, New York: Free Press.

Wilson, D. C. (1980) 'Organizational Strategy', Ph.D. thesis, University of Bradford Management Centre, Bradford.

Wilson, D. C. and Rosenfeld, R. H. (1990) *Managing Organizations: Text, Readings and Cases*, London and New York: McGraw-Hill.

Wilson, D. C., Butler, R. J., Cray, D., Hickson, D. J., and Mallory, G. R. (1986) 'Breaking the bounds of organization in strategic decision-making', *Human Relations* 39, 4:309–31.

Wolff, J. (1977) 'Women in organizations', in S. Clegg and D. Dunkerley (eds) *Critical Issues in Organizations*, London: Routledge.

Zuboff, S. (1988) *In the Age of the Smart Machine*, Oxford: Heinemann.

Index